From a Nickel to a Token

From a Nickel to a Token

The *Journey* From BOARD OF TRANSPORTATION TO MTA

ANDREW J. SPARBERG

ESE

EMPIRE STATE EDITIONS
AN IMPRINT OF FORDHAM UNIVERSITY PRESS
NEW YORK 2015

Library of Congress Cataloging-in-Publication Data is available from the publisher.

Printed in the United States of America

17   16   15   5   4   3   2   1

First edition

For Donna

Contents

Preface *ix*

Acknowledgments *xi*

1. 1940: Unification—IRT and BMT Join the IND,
   Creating One Subway System *1*

2. 1941: A Strike and a Pioneering Labor Agreement *16*

3. 1941: Dyre Avenue Subway Extension Opens *25*

4. 1941–1948: Third Avenue Transit—Rails to Rubber *31*

5. 1944 and 1950: Goodbye to Brooklyn Bridge Rails *42*

6. 1947–1948: Private to Public Bus Operations *49*

7. 1948: Goodbye to the Nickel *59*

8. 1947–1956: Final Decade for Brooklyn Trolleys *67*

9. 1950: Farewell, Lexington Avenue *75*

10. 1953–1968: The TA, Tokens, and TWU Triumphant *80*

11. 1953: Last Double-Deck Buses Operate on Fifth Avenue *96*

12. 1954–1956: The BMT and IND Begin a Courtship *100*

13. 1955: Sunshine Returns to Third Avenue *111*

14. 1956: Fifth Avenue Coach Becomes Number One *117*

15. 1957–1959: IRT West Side Improvement *122*

16. 1962: Fifth Avenue Coach Suddenly Disappears *129*

17. 1964: World's Fair, Blue Subways, Stainless Steel Subways *137*

18. 1966: Mike Quill's Last Hurrah *143*

19. 1967: The BMT and IND Marry Forever *151*

20. 1968: The MTA Is Created and Express Buses Appear *159*

Bibliography *167*

Index *169*

In 1940 mass transit providers in major U.S. and Canadian cities were, with a few exceptions, privately owned concerns, typically one large company operating under municipal franchise rights. New York, because of its vast size, was home to a multitude of private subway, elevated, streetcar, and bus concerns; it also had one large publicly owned network, the Independent Subway System (IND).

This pattern changed beginning in 1940. That year, New York's city government bought out its two huge private subway-elevated companies, the Interborough Rapid Transit (IRT) and Brooklyn-Manhattan Transit (BMT). The latter also encompassed Brooklyn's large streetcar and bus network. The IRT and BMT were unified with the IND to create a citywide rapid transit network under one management. Between 1947 and 1962 most bus operations in all five boroughs were folded into the citywide system as well. This pattern was repeated in virtually the entire U.S. and Canadian mass transit industry as well, so by the mid-1970s privately owned mass transit systems had disappeared in all but a few locales.

In 1968 a New York State agency, the Metropolitan Transportation Authority (MTA), was created to oversee not only New York City's subway and bus system but also the commuter railroad network wholly within New York State and the toll bridges and tunnels within the five boroughs. Some years later I would embark on a twenty-five-year career at one of the MTA's agencies.

This book is an examination of twenty specific events in the history of New York's mass transit system during that 1940–1968 period, bookended by the subway unification and the MTA's creation. It is not a comprehensive history, as other authors have written such works. The events depicted are a mixture of well-remembered, partially forgotten, and totally obscure happenings that represent pieces of the larger and fascinating historical tapestry of New York City mass transit. The city's mayors during this period—Fiorello LaGuardia, William O'Dwyer, Vincent Impellitteri, Robert Wagner, and John Lindsay—all devoted much energy to solving transit issues and appeasing the riding public, their fellow elected officials, transit system managements, and labor leaders.

The book includes a large number of photos of the transit system during the 1940–1968 period, many of which have never been published. The photos in turn document a city that has changed and is forever undergoing further changes.

From the end of World War II until 1968 the Board of Transportation and its successor, the New York City Transit Authority, concentrated on replacing worn-out rolling stock with new cars and buses and rehabilitating basic infrastructure—stations, signals, tracks, and power systems. The last streetcars ran in 1956. One new rapid transit branch line was added (to Rockaway, Queens), and a number of short strategic connections were built in all four subway boroughs to permit through-train services to operate wherever possible. In 1947–1948 private bus operators in Staten Island, eastern Queens, and one portion of Manhattan became public sector operations. In 1962 the largest remaining private bus operator, serving Manhattan and the Bronx, moved into the public fold after a sudden labor dispute. After that year only Queens had a significant collection of private bus companies.

While significant progress had been made by the mid-1960s to preserve and improve the subway and bus systems, public officials in New York determined that mass transit was destined to be a complete public and regional responsibility. Recognizing that the increasingly dispersed populations of both New York City and its surrounding suburbs created mobility demands that did not stop at the city limits, New York State's political leadership determined that a new agency was needed to fold the subways and buses into something bigger.

Accordingly, in 1968 the subways and the public sector bus networks in all five boroughs were combined into a new public agency, the New York State Metropolitan Transportation Authority, today universally known as the MTA. Its mandate was to unify the overall planning and financing for all mass transportation services in a twelve-county region encompassing New York City's boroughs, five counties in the Hudson Valley, and two counties on Long Island. The highway crossings of the Triborough Bridge and Tunnel Authority were also included. For the first time, virtually all public transit on the New York side of the Hudson River—bus, subway, and commuter rail—came under a single agency management, which has continued for nearly half a century since then.

As I was researching, writing, and editing this work, it became obvious that mass transit is not an end unto itself. It reflects overall life in the metropolis, as evidenced by the photographs that not only show subways and buses but also the city. So a secondary purpose of this book is for the photographs to show the changing city itself during this period. While it is often stated that New York cannot function without its mass transit system, the fact is that mass transit needs the city in order to function effectively. If few or no people ride transit, it quickly disappears.

So join me on a historical trip back to both well-remembered and long-forgotten events, when a five-cent rise in the transit fare was enough to provoke many lines of newspaper copy and much commentary and analysis on radio and television.

Acknowledgments

Many people contributed to the publication of *From a Nickel to a Token*. The two most important are Fred Nachbaur, director of Fordham University Press, and Gabrielle Shubert, director of the New York Transit Museum. Without them, this book would never have been written.

Fred introduced himself to me at the 2010 New York State History Conference in Ithaca, where I delivered a paper about the history of the former Long Island Rail Road Rockaway Beach Line, now part of the A train subway route. Upon hearing about my long association with the New York Transit Museum, Fred asked if I would be interested in writing a book in conjunction with the museum. After I developed the outline for this book, Fred was instrumental in getting the necessary corporate approvals quickly and expeditiously. He was enthusiastic, from the very beginning, about writing a selective history of specific transit-related events, using photographic material that has mostly been unpublished until now.

Gabrielle Shubert was kind enough to grant me full access to the museum's extensive photo archives, a critical factor in producing this volume. Carey Stumm and Desiree Alden of the museum's archive office were unhesitatingly generous with their time as I sifted through photo after photo in search of the materials used in this book. Thanks to their assistance and cooperation, the majority of the photos herein are being published for the first time.

The Transport Workers Union Local 100 publications director, Alan Saly, graciously allowed me to access the union's archives when I phoned. Thanks to him, additional unique photos are now within these covers. The Queens Museum of the Arts provided two photos of the 1964 World's Fair.

Fred Eisinger of the Motor Bus Society was kind enough to meet me at the Trenton, New Jersey, rail station and drive me to the MBS photo archive office in nearby Hopewell, where we spent the better part of a day examining and scanning bus photos, many of which appear herein as well.

Joe Cunningham, Eddie Crew, and Bob Presbrey were also very generous with their time. Joe is a colleague from CUNY's School of Professional Studies, Eddie is a retired subway conductor with an encyclopedic knowledge of the whole transit system, and Bob is a colleague from my Long Island Rail Road career whose knowledge of Brooklyn's vanished trolleys and elevateds is second to no one. Joe read the entire manuscript, and Eddie and Bob reviewed many chapters and photo captions. All provided useful comments, suggestions, and corrections. Tammy Raum of the New York City Law Department located the legal citation that created the Manhattan and Bronx

Surface Transit Operating Authority in 1962. Joe Raskin, author of *The Routes Not Taken*, read the final manuscript and provided positive and useful comments.

Thanks are also owed to Fordham Press staff members Wil Cerbone, Katie Sweeney, and Kate O'Brien-Nicholson for their assistance.

The remaining acknowledgments are personal. My late father, Lester, and my mother, Esther, deserve recognition for encouraging my lifelong interest in transportation, dating back to our original home at Riverside Drive and 104th Street. And saving the best for last, my charming and beautiful wife Donna has always been supportive, literally from the very beginning, when on our first date when we took a Columbus Avenue bus to catch a movie at a midtown theater. A Bronx native who herself has never kicked the mass transit habit, Donna was enthusiastic when I channeled my lifelong interest in transportation into a career at the MTA Long Island Rail Road, where I spent twenty-five years of a forty-year odyssey that is still moving along. She learned in those LIRR years, being a railroad wife is not always easy, especially when balancing her own demanding career as a college professor and additional roles as a daughter, mother, and now grandmother. So it is Donna to whom this book is dedicated.

From a Nickel to a Token

1940: Unification

1

Over a twelve-day period in June 1940, the City of New York purchased the two privately operated subway companies, the Brooklyn-Manhattan Transit Company (BMT) and the Interborough Rapid Transit Company (IRT). The total cost, $326 million, was financed by municipal bonds paying 3 percent interest. The two companies became the BMT and IRT Divisions, respectively, of the now-unified New York City Transit System (hence the term, "unification"), joining the Independent Subway System, owned and operated by the City of New York from its inception in 1924; the latter now became the IND division. The Board of Transportation, a city agency reporting directly to Mayor Fiorello LaGuardia, was responsible for operating and maintaining the entire system, which also included an extensive bus and streetcar system in Brooklyn that was inherited with the BMT purchase.[1]

The Board of Transportation will be referred to many times in this book. New York State created it in 1924 to empower the City of New York to build and operate the Independent Subway System (IND). The Board of Transportation greatly expanded in 1940 when under subway unification it added the IRT and BMT to its domain. In 1947 and 1948, when private bus operators in Staten Island, Queens, and Manhattan were bought, its stable of operations once again increased. In 1953 the Board of Transportation was abolished; its replacement was the New York City Transit Authority, still in existence today.

LaGuardia had an ambivalent attitude toward mass transit.[2] He was in agreement with the Robert Moses mentality that automobiles and highways were destined to be the dominant transport modes in the future, which was consistent with his embrace of aviation. At the same time, never forgetting that he was still a politician, the mayor recognized that two-thirds of New York households did not own automobiles in 1940, and thus he did not ignore a mass transit system's importance to the well-being of New Yorkers. He was unabashedly in favor of retaining the nickel fare, which was one of

---

1. Clifton Hood, 722 Miles (Baltimore, Md.: Johns Hopkins University Press, 1993), 205.

2. Ibid., 226–227. Mayor LaGuardia is described as feeling that the subway system was a source of potential difficulty (read: fare increases) and that it represented old-fashioned technology. The mayor clearly backed Robert Moses's bridge and highway projects of the 1930s and considered the automobile the transportation mode of the future.

unification's key selling points. So when unification did occur, the media considered it a positive event. The headline from the *New York Times*, June 14, 1940, announces the conclusion of a twenty-plus-year campaign, going back to John Hylan's mayoralty, to create a single, unified New York subway system.

New York Times (left) February 25, 1940 and (right) June 14, 1940.

In 1940 the Board of Transportation became the largest, and one of the few, publicly owned mass transit systems in North America, comprising 250 route miles of subway and elevated lines, plus another three hundred route miles of bus and streetcar lines. The Dual Contracts agreements of 1913, which created the modern BMT and IRT subway networks, were based on a premise that the two companies' fare revenues would create enough money to pay the interest on city bonds originally issued to build the vast new subway system between 1913 and 1931.[3] The fares never came close to raising the money needed, so the city itself paid those interest charges out of tax revenues. According to the historian Clifton Hood, between 1919 and 1940 the city only received $2.1 million from the IRT's operating revenues and nothing from the BMT. The result was that the city incurred a total accumulated deficit of $461 million over that twenty-one-year period, which was covered from general tax revenues.[4]

It should be noted that the BMT as a corporate entity was created in 1923. Prior to that it was known as the Brooklyn Rapid Transit Company (BRT). The name was changed to

3. The Dual Contracts refers to a pair of agreements signed in March 1913 between the City of New York and two private rapid transit companies, the Interborough Rapid Transit (IRT) and Brooklyn Rapid Transit (BRT), hence the term "dual." In return for the city financing construction of new subways and elevated extensions in all boroughs except Staten Island, the two companies agreed to operate their systems under a forty-nine-year lease charging a five-cent fare.

4. Hood, *722 Miles*, 195.

BMT when the firm emerged from a five-year period of receivership, partially because of a fatal train 1918 accident at Prospect Park that killed ninety-three people.[5]

Unification had been discussed since 1921, when Mayor John Hylan proposed "recapture" of some Dual Contracts routes into a single, municipally owned subway system. In 1924 a municipal system became reality when the Board of Transportation was created to build and operate the new Independent Subway System (IND), which was constructed beginning in 1925 and opened in stages between 1932 and 1940. The IND was deliberately built to be physically compatible with the BMT, so that future train routes could include parts of both the BMT and IND. Proponents of unification believed that significant economies of scale could be achieved by merging the three subway operators. Another benefit would be eliminating many costly, duplicative, and functionally obsolete nineteenth-century elevated train operations in Manhattan and Brooklyn, where newer IND and BMT subway routes paralleled the old routes. The hoped-for result would be for the system to reduce its financial problems and be less of a drain on the city treasury. The fare would remain at five cents until 1948, a political and psychological barrier that was tough to break (see Chapter 7).

An example of how the nickel fare was a hot-button issue in the late thirties and early forties can be gleaned from the classic guidebook *WPA Guide to New York City*, published in 1939. A chapter about the subway and elevated lines concludes with the sentences: "The five cent fare—a recurring issue in municipal politics—is not likely to be increased in the immediate or distant future. The New Yorker is extremely sensitive on this point."[6] How true, seventy-plus years later. Though the nickel by itself nowadays is essentially worthless, today's transit fare is no less sensitive a political issue.

Whatever the case, the Board of Transportation was now faced with a number of daunting tasks. The *New York Times* published an article on February 25, 1940, about four months prior to the actual implementation of the unified subway system. The piece was an insightful analysis about the challenges the newly unified system would face—complex operating, labor, and financial problems. Today these issues are still very much on the front burner. Only the dollar amounts are higher because of inflation.

Operating issues were both short and long term. The former needed immediate examination because the elimination of old elevated routes required the creation of free transfers where newer IND subways replaced four old BMT and IRT elevated routes that closed immediately upon unification in June 1940. Two were BMT routes in Brooklyn along Fifth and Third Avenues (between downtown and 65th Street) and Fulton Street (between downtown and Rockaway Avenue). Two were IRT routes in Manhattan

5. Brian Cudahy, *Under the Sidewalks of New York* (New York: Fordham University Press, 1995), 80.

6. Federal Writers Project, *WPA Guide to New York City* (New York, Federal Writers Project, 1939), 406.

Two views of Second Avenue El trains from Queens (Astoria or Flushing) that have just crossed the Queensboro Bridge before going south above Second Avenue to complete trips to South Ferry. The image on the left looks south from the 60th Street side of the bridge. The image on the right looks north at a southbound train that has just crossed the bridge. Note how the structure rises high over the southbound tracks from upper Manhattan. Both photos were taken in approximately 1940, when the Board of Transportation took over the IRT. This line was razed in 1942. Since then there has been no one-seat service between the IRT Flushing Line and Lower Manhattan. Source: New York Transit Museum Archives. All subsequent photos from the New York Transit Museum Archives will be identified as "NYTM" only with a specific collection included if appropriate.

along Second Avenue north of 57th Street and along Ninth Avenue south of 155th Street. All four routes had parallel subway or elevated routes within one block and thus were a good example of the types of cost savings that unification would achieve. Interdivisional transfers were created at locations where IND subway customers had to continue trips on older elevated routes. These locations were 155th Street in Manhattan (to the IRT Polo Grounds Shuttle), 161st Street in the Bronx (to the IRT Jerome Avenue Line), Franklin Avenue in Brooklyn (to the BMT Franklin Shuttle), and Rockaway Avenue in Brooklyn (to the BMT Fulton Street Elevated). Prior to unification the only intercompany transfer was at Queensboro Plaza, where the IRT and BMT already operated a joint station. Otherwise, transfer privileges were not expanded where two or more divisions intersected; this would not occur until the 1948 fare increase.

Elevated Lines Explained

At this juncture a short explanation of elevated lines would be appropriate. Between 1870 and 1900 Manhattan and Brooklyn developed two separate, steam-powered elevated train systems. All were electrified in the first years of the twentieth century. The Manhattan els, which also included the Third Avenue Line in the Bronx, became an operating entity of the IRT subway through a long-term lease. The Brooklyn els became a part of the BMT's rapid transit network, and some of its early routes were rebuilt and connected to the subways.

During the 1930s there was considerable pressure to remove many nineteenth-century elevated train routes in Brooklyn and Manhattan. Most required the use of wood-bodied equipment because the structures were never upgraded to permit operation of modern steel subway cars. The noise and blight associated with the elevateds was also blamed for low property values on the affected streets. The IND subway was built in part to replace a number of el routes. In Manhattan, the new Sixth and Eighth Avenue subways replaced IRT els on Sixth and Ninth

Ninth Avenue El at 110th Street and Eighth Avenue, spring 1940, looking northwest. The double-decker bus is a Fifth Avenue Coach vehicle going uptown on either the #3 or #4 routes to Washington Heights. The train is traveling between Lower Manhattan and either 155th Street or Woodlawn (Bronx). Although the el has been gone for over seventy years, buses continue to serve these routes. NYTM

Second and Third Avenue El, 1940, near the South Ferry terminal at Coenties Slip. Second Avenue trains used this stretch until 1942; Third Avenue trains would use it until 1950, when it was razed. NYTM

Avenues. In Brooklyn, the Fulton Street subway replaced the BMT el on the same street, practically block by block. In 1915 one of the first Dual Contracts subways, the BMT route under Brooklyn's Fourth Avenue, was a block from the BMT's older Fifth–Third Avenue elevated route.

Between 1938 and 1973, all pre-1900 elevated routes in Manhattan, the Bronx, and Brooklyn were razed, with two exceptions. Those are the J and M routes in Brooklyn, which still use structures built between 1885 and 1893 for steam trains. The remaining elevated rapid transit routes in New York were built as part of the Dual Contracts subway expansions between 1915 and 1922 and are not considered elevated lines in the New York context.

The Second Avenue El in Manhattan south of 57th Street to Chatham Square was initially retained as it connected to tracks that crossed the Queensboro Bridge, connecting the el to the Astoria and Flushing lines in Queens. But pressure to eliminate the Second Avenue El caused this route to be closed completely on June 13, 1942. This move reduced by two tracks rapid transit linkage between Queens and Manhattan, which became an issue in the 1950s, when Queens experienced much residential growth. It also eliminated a one-seat ride between the Flushing Line and Lower Manhattan, something still not possible today. After 1942, the only remaining nineteenth-century elevated on Manhattan was on Third Avenue, and it would last only another thirteen years.

The long-term operating issues involved the need to rationalize subway routings, including constructing short links where IND subway trains could provide through service on older BMT Brooklyn elevated routes. A look at a 1940 map shows many logical routes that could be created by building links between the IND and BMT networks.

Since the IND was built with the same clearances as the BMT, such links would create a more efficient subway-elevated system. Two obvious links involved IND subways in Brooklyn. In 1940 the A line ended at Rockaway Avenue, and the F line ended at Church Avenue. Both lines would ultimately be extended along former BMT elevated routes after World War II. In 1940, A train passengers had to transfer between the IND and BMT at Rockaway Avenue but could make the entire trip to or from Lefferts Boulevard for a single fare. In 1956 the entire line became a single route from Manhattan to Lefferts Boulevard. On the F train, passengers were stranded at Church Avenue until the old Culver Elevated was connected to the IND. A ramp between Church and Ditmas Avenues that provided this link was actually under construction in 1941 when World War II stopped the work; it did not open for revenue service until October 1954 and was then part of the D train route. Chapter 12 gives more details about this and other related BMT-IND linkages.

The BMT originally had a whole stable of el lines that began at the Park Row terminal (opposite City Hall in Lower Manhattan), crossed the Brooklyn Bridge, and then fanned out after reaching the Brooklyn side. The el routes along Fulton Street, Fifth and Third Avenues, Lexington Avenue, and Myrtle Avenue survived into the unification era. Additional el routes that became today's Coney Island subway lines (the Brighton, Culver, Sea Beach, and West End lines) originally accessed downtown Brooklyn and Lower Manhattan via the Fulton or Fifth Avenue el routes and the Brooklyn Bridge. With the advent of the Dual Contracts, new subway routes over the Manhattan Bridge and along Flatbush and Fourth Avenues allowed these older el routes to be rebuilt into grade-separated rapid transit routes, replacing the earlier Brooklyn Bridge routing.

After unification, and the elimination of the Fulton Street and Fifth–Third Avenue els, Brooklyn Bridge el routes were whittled down to the Myrtle and Lexington lines. In 1941 the Board of Transportation proposed to eliminate the bridge el tracks, truncate both routes at Jay Street in downtown Brooklyn, and move the Brooklyn Bridge streetcar lines to the former el tracks in the middle of the bridge. The purpose was to provide more room for motor vehicles and improve highway approaches on both sides. The el trains did stop running in March 1944, and scrap metal from the old terminals on the Manhattan and Brooklyn sides was used for the World War II efforts. El passengers wishing to continue over the Brooklyn Bridge were given a free paper transfer to the bridge streetcar routes, which continued operating using the former el tracks. In 1950, as part of a rebuilding of the Brooklyn Bridge for auto traffic only, the bridge streetcars were eliminated. Chapter 5 provides details of the Brooklyn Bridge rail eliminations.

Another operating issue was the Board of Transportation's inheritance of the BMT's large surface transport system in Brooklyn, encompassing three hundred route miles, 1,700 streetcars, five hundred gasoline buses, and ten trolley buses. The routes covered all corners of Brooklyn, extended deep into Queens, and touched Manhattan. One long-term operating question was whether the system would remain streetcar dominated.

Mayor LaGuardia was unabashedly opposed to streetcars; he favored rubber-tired surface transit. In 1936, the BMT introduced one hundred new, modern President's Conference Committee (PCC) streetcars on three Brooklyn routes—Smith–Coney Island, McDonald–Vanderbilt, and Erie Basin. Despite their operating success and immediate public acceptance, in 1938 LaGuardia prevented the BMT from purchasing an additional five hundred modern PCC streetcars to replace older rolling stock (he used the impending BMT purchase by the city to convince federal officials to back away from granting the BMT a U.S. government loan for the car purchase). With the surface system now in city hands after June 1940, it was no secret that ultimately Brooklyn's surface lines would be 100 percent buses, although target dates kept changing. In the years right after World War II, the Board of Transportation replaced many miles of streetcar tracks, only to convert some of its heaviest lines (Flatbush and Nostrand Avenues, for example) to bus in 1951.

Chapter 8 covers in detail Brooklyn's streetcar-to-bus conversions between 1947 and 1956. Throughout this book the terms "streetcar" and "trolley" are used interchangeably, both referring to electric-powered surface transit vehicles. New York was unique because it had both conventional overhead wire systems (in Brooklyn, the Bronx, and Queens) and a unique Manhattan system featuring an underground electrical conduit to supply power. "Trolley" also refers to the pole that connects the vehicle to its overhead electric power supply, meaning that Manhattan's lines should only be called "streetcars."

Mayor LaGuardia, The PCC Cars, and Buses

Mayor LaGuardia's ascension to power in 1934 occurred just as the U.S. urban transit industry was developing a new streetcar design that would stem the tide of passenger losses from bus and private automobile competition. LaGuardia's anti-streetcar bias did not prevent the PCC car from being introduced in New York, but it played a big role in the eventual elimination of all streetcars from New York's streets.

In 1929 the presidents of the major streetcar companies, including the BMT, conferred at an Atlantic City hotel and formed the Electric Railway Presidents' Conference Committee (PCC). The committee's goal was to design a new and modern type of streetcar that would attract passengers and reflect technological developments of the 1920s. A detailed research program was created, and extensive fieldwork was done, with the BMT itself volunteering to be a laboratory to test new components. The committee arranged for a sample car to be built, and it was tested on the BMT's network in 1934. The new PCC design was deemed successful, and a new business entity called the Transit Research Corporation (TRC) was created to protect the committee's design patents.

The Electric Railway Presidents' Conference Committee expired in 1936, when the first new PCC cars came off the production lines. Since the BMT played such an active role in PCC car development, it was only fitting that the BMT obtained the first mass production order of one hundred cars. The first ones entered service in October 1936 on the Smith Street–Coney Island Avenue route. The cars were an immediate success, and soon there was pressure for the

BMT to order additional units to begin replacement of its older equipment. Brooklyn was still a streetcar stronghold in 1936.

Mayor Fiorello LaGuardia, on the other hand, harbored anti-streetcar sentiments before the PCC cars hit the streets and was not swayed sufficiently to change his mind. Upon ascending to City Hall in January 1934, LaGuardia made it clear that his surface transportation policy was twofold—a small group of large operating companies focused on one borough, and the ultimate conversion of all routes from streetcars to buses. The first test came in Manhattan early in 1935. The Fifth Avenue Coach Company, the first U.S. urban bus operator, had taken control of the very large New York Railways (NYR) streetcar network in 1926, with the ultimate goal of converting the network to buses. In 1934 General Motors developed buses with the new technology of rear-mounted engines, which permitted sufficient seating capacity to operate on streetcar routes. With LaGuardia's blessing, between February 1935 and July 1936 Fifth Avenue Coach formed a subsidiary (New York City Omnibus Corporation, or NYCO) and installed a fleet of over seven hundred new General Motors buses on the former NYR routes. On January 29, 1935, two days before NYCO buses replaced the Madison Avenue streetcars, LaGuardia delivered a radio speech and was quoted in the *New York Times* the following day as saying "trolleys are as dead as sailing ships." He also declared that substituting buses for streetcars was the policy of his administration.

So by the time the BMT introduced the PCC car LaGuardia's anti-streetcar sentiments were public knowledge. The cars' threefold Brooklyn success (with company management, employees, and the riding public) was so strong that in April 1938 the BMT obtained conditional approval for a U.S. government (Reconstruction Finance Corporation) loan to purchase five hundred more new PCC cars. Had these cars been obtained, there is no doubt that Brooklyn would have remained a streetcar stronghold into the 1960s. However, the proposal died in September 1938 when Mayor LaGuardia's opposition led to the rescinding of the loan approval.[7] Because of LaGuardia's stubbornness, the initial PCC cars of 1936 were the only ones ever to operate in New York City.

LaGuardia's feelings continued to be well known after his 1947 death. In January 1955, the New York City Transit Authority's house organ *Transit*, in an article about the impending end of Brooklyn streetcar service, reiterated that LaGuardia's opposition to the 1938 RFC loan ended any hopes of additional PCC cars on Brooklyn streets. The last PCCs closed out Brooklyn's streetcar era on October 31, 1956, when the cars completed their runs on the Church and McDonald Avenue lines.

The Board of Transportation wasted no time implementing its pro-bus policy. Two hundred and fifty new buses, leased from the Twin Coach Company of Kent, Ohio, for $3.5 million, were delivered in 1941 to replace streetcars on six Brooklyn routes—Fulton Street, Gates Avenue, Putnam Avenue, Third Avenue, New Lots Avenue, and Hamilton Avenue. DeKalb Avenue, originally a candidate for conversion, remained a rail route after World War II started in December 1941, in order to retain enough buses for the

---

7. *New York Times* (September 28, 1938).

#1101 of Brooklyn's new bus fleet was snapped covering a B25/Fulton Street route assignment on August 11, 1941, picking up passengers for an eastbound trip from downtown Brooklyn. NYTM

other routes, as the war put an end to bus production for civilian customers. Putnam Avenue was converted back to streetcars in November 1942 to reduce bus usage to comply with U.S. government wartime restrictions to save petroleum fuels and rubber. So while the bus was making inroads in the Borough of Churches, the streetcar was not exactly disappearing.

The bus conversion was not without controversy. The Citizen's Budget Commission, a watchdog group, sued the Board of Transportation in December 1940 to stop the lease, on the grounds that it was an unconstitutional means of getting around the city's mandated debt limit for issuing bonds for capital improvements. It took a new state law, passed in March 1941, which allowed the city to lease the buses, to end the lawsuit threat. The buses were urgently needed not only because of the planned streetcar conversions but because the Fulton Street elevated line, abandoned when the city took over the BMT under unification, was still standing in downtown Brooklyn, and the streetcars could not operate without the wires that were suspended from its structure. Removing the el without bus substitution on the Futon, Gates, and Putnam lines would force the use of temporary poles and wires to permit continued streetcar operation. In May 1941 the first of the new, leased buses appeared, as reported in the *New York Times* of May 17. A smiling mayor was quoted telling Board of Transportation and Twin Coach officials to "keep them [the buses] coming."

World War II's fuel and rubber shortages and the relative newness of many streetcars ensured that Brooklyn surface routes would remain rail based for quite a while. After 1947 the streetcar-to-bus conversions resumed in earnest, and they are discussed in more detail in Chapter 8.

Shown in 1941 are two 8000 series double-ended Peter Witt type cars, #8111 and behind it #8129, both on the long Ocean Avenue Line on a snowy day. The cars are on Farragut Road heading geographically east as they transition from Ocean to Rogers Avenues on northbound runs to Bergen Street. NYTM, Lonto-Watson Collection

Shown in 1940, on Court Street in downtown Brooklyn after a snowfall, are two cars. An 8000 series double-ended Peter Witt type car, #8192, is on the Third Avenue Line, and behind it is a still new PCC headed to the Brooklyn Bridge on either the Smith–Coney Island or Seventh Avenue Line. One of the many Chock Full o' Nuts restaurants is on the right. NYTM, Lonto-Watson Collection

The following seven photos of streetcars were all taken in the periods before and after the unification and show a large streetcar network that was entering the winter of its life. Some pictures are actually in Queens since some of the BMT's streetcars extended into that borough.

The labor relations issues were daunting also. The multitude of work rules and job classifications on the two private legacy systems and the city-owned IND would need to be consolidated, clarified, and rewritten for the new unified system, along with ex- isting agreements with the Transport Workers Union (TWU). In 1937, the IRT and BMT systems had negotiated labor agreements with the TWU that mandated a closed shop for all covered employees. While the TWU also represented IND workers as well, as unification loomed on the horizon it was not clear whether the city would honor the IRT and BMT agreements. Realizing that, the TWU's 1939 agreements with the IRT and BMT were written to remain effective until June 30, 1941, a year after unification would occur.[8]

Because New York City owned and operated the IND from its 1932 inception, its employees were also covered under New York City's civil service law provisions. Meld- ing the BMT and IRT's workers into the civil service system opened up a host of new issues that created new fissures in Albany between upstate and downstate legislators. In the spring of 1939 a Republican state senator from Kingston, Arthur H. Wicks, intro- duced a law that would force the BMT and IRT workers to lose their private company

8. Joshua B. Freeman, *In Transit* (New York: Oxford University Press, 1989), 187–191.

Peter Witt–type car #8276 is shown on the Third Avenue Line in 1941, as demolition of the old elevated line continued. The pillars would be reused to support the new Robert Moses highway, the Gowanus Parkway. Buses replaced the cars in 1941. NYTM, Lonto-Watson Collection

6000 series car #6086 is shown around 1941 at the Flushing end of the Flushing-Ridgewood Line, about to turn onto Main Street and begin a return trip. Behind is #8590. Ad on #6086 is for Bond Bread; billboard at right advertises Heinz Tomato Soup. NYTM, Mordetsky Collection

seniority and go into the New York City civil service system if and when unification occurred. In addition, any workers who were not U.S. citizens would not be allowed to work for the future city-owned system, a major problem for the many Irish-born TWU members who had not become naturalized.

For many months in the first half of 1939, the Wicks law was a matter of heated debate in Albany and New York City. The TWU lobbied strongly to defeat the law, realizing that its newly won gains could evaporate after municipal ownership. The law was finally passed and signed by Governor Lehman in June 1939, weaker than its original provisions but still potentially a problem for the TWU's IRT and BMT workers. Accordingly, the TWU lobbied Mayor LaGuardia to ensure that, when unification occurred, those workers would keep their seniority and job titles. Furthermore, the citizenship requirement was amended to allow a sworn intention to become a citizen. LaGuardia and the TWU reached agreement on these issues, after some difficult negotiations, in April 1940, heading off any disastrous work stoppage when unification became reality.[9] From the TWU's standpoint, it was a watershed—it would maintain its position as the dominant labor organization in the New York City mass transit industry, a position it maintains to this day.

On the financial side, the Board of Transportation now faced the challenge of upgrading and modernizing the BMT and IRT divisions, which despite their relative youth (the oldest portions of the subways were then thirty-six years old) were in physical decline. Some rolling stock needed replacement, and stations needed work. World War II's onset in December 1941 put the brakes on any immediate plans to upgrade the system, which

9. Ibid., 200.

would gain additional riders but suffer from undermaintenance during the next four years. The war threw millions of additional riders onto the system thanks to full employment and restrictions on private auto use after gasoline and tire rationing. At the same time the Board of Transportation's work force was being depleted as men went into military service, and obtaining replacement workers became a problem.

The war also granted a temporary respite from the fare debates and created a temporary spike in operating revenues that would not last. The New York City transit system managed to cover its operating costs from the nickel tariff during the war and even generated a surplus. This result caused Mayor LaGuardia to proclaim that "we got a good deal" when referring to the city's IRT and BMT purchase in 1940.[10] As an example: in the first full fiscal year of Board of Transportation operation, the system generated $114.8 million in fare revenues, versus $87.4 million in operating expenses, leaving a surplus of $27.4 million, which was used to pay off some of the interest and amortization charges on city bonds issued to pay for the BMT and IRT purchases.[11] If that revenue were not available, such charges would have to be paid from direct tax revenues.

While LaGuardia's claim was justified at the time, it was also shortsighted. After he left office at the beginning of 1946, the end of the war, recurring inflation, and changing demographics saw the nickel fare finally end amid long-term issues of physical plant and rolling stock replacement, fares and finances, and service levels. Each issue became a perennial problem, ones still debated in the twenty-first century.

Timeline of Major Urban Transit Systems' Entering Public Sector			
CITY	**YEAR(S)**	**CITY OR STATE**	**YEAR(S)**
San Francisco	1912, 1944	Los Angeles	1958
Seattle	1919	Oakland	1960
Toronto	1921	Pittsburgh	1964
Detroit	1922	St. Louis	1964
New York	1932, 1940, 1947, 1948, 1962, 1980, 2006	Philadelphia	1968, 1970
Cleveland	1942	Baltimore	1970
Chicago	1947, 1952	Washington	1973
Boston	1947, 1964	New Jersey	1980
Montreal	1951	New Orleans	1983

10. Hood, *722 Miles*, 100.
11. *New York Times* (November 17, 1941).

#8321 is working the Grand Street Line on Junction Boulevard in Corona, Queens, about 1941. The LIRR Port Washington Branch is above, with one of the famous MP54 arched-roof MU trains. NYTM, Mordetsky Collection

Lineup of PCC cars at West 5th Street Depot, Coney Island, about 1941. The cars on left and right are on the #69 McDonald–Vanderbilt Avenues Line; in the center is the #68 Smith Street–Coney Island Avenue Line. NYTM, Mordetsky Collection

Lineup of cars in downtown Brooklyn about 1941, near Borough Hall. The Fulton Street el, overhead, is being razed. A 6000 series car is in the right foreground on the Gates Avenue Line; an 8000 series car on the Third Avenue Line is passing it going toward Bay Ridge. Both lines would be converted to bus soon after this photo was taken. On the right are two of the ubiquitous DeSoto taxicabs of that era, near a branch of Wallach's, a quality men's store that lasted until the 1970s. NYTM, Mordetsky Collection

Once unification was a reality, New York City's Board of Transportation dwarfed earlier publicly owned urban transit systems in San Francisco, Detroit, Toronto, and Seattle—all of which then involved surface vehicles only and did not include any subway or elevated lines. But the writing was on the wall. In 1947 the Boston and Chicago systems, both of which included extensive subway and elevated routes, became public sector responsibilities. Although it could not be foreseen in 1940, New York's subway unification was the beginning of a forty-year trend that saw all urban transport in the United States move into the public sector. The last holdouts, New Jersey's statewide bus and rail systems and the streetcar and bus system in New Orleans, finally came into public ownership in the 1980s. The accompanying table shows, for selected large North American cities, the years when mass transit systems became public sector responsibilities. Cities where multiple years appear mean that different segments of the overall

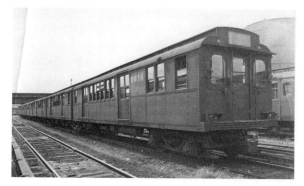

At the time of the 1940 unification, each subway operator had its own unique type of car equipment. The BMT division car shown here is a 1927-vintage Triplex unit that normally operated on the Brighton and Sea Beach Lines. It was unique because the cars were arranged in three-section units, with an articulated truck between the first/second and second/third cars of each unit. NYTM

The most numerous BMT cars at the time of unification and for years afterward were the sixty-seven-foot "Standard" car, built between 1915 and 1924. Its size and design could accommodate heavy crowds. NYTM

system were taken over in different years. In the cases of San Francisco (1912) and New York (1932), those two years refer to when entirely new, city-owned systems first went into service.

A final historical fact should be noted. Unification occurred during the second summer of the New York World's Fair. The IND, BMT, IRT, and Long Island Rail Road all provided rail service to the Flushing Meadows fair site, as did numerous privately owned bus routes. The IND service ran over a new track extension built especially for the fair; the other three systems used existing tracks.[12] The only trolley route that served the fair site was the BMT's Flushing–Ridgewood car, which became part of the Board of Transportation after unification. The World's Fair subway services continued to operate without interruption until closing day, October 27, 1940, the only difference being that IRT and BMT subway and trolley customers were riding on a city-owned system. The IND's World's Fair service, a temporary branch from the Queens Boulevard sub-

12. This line was not retained after 1940, and the tracks were removed. Today the right-of-way is part of the Van Wyck Expressway north of Kew Gardens and south of the Long Island Expressway.

The IRT's 1940 car fleet is represented by this photo, which was actually taken in the early 1950s. It shows a Dyre Avenue Line train in the Bronx, headed by a 1939-vintage World's Fair car, so called because it was one of fifty units built to provide added service to that event. NYTM

The most typical IRT equipment of the postunification era was the Low-V car, which was found all over the IRT's two main trunk routes: Seventh Avenue–Broadway and Lexington Avenue. NYTM

The IND division, always city owned and operated, had a fleet of 1,703 nearly identical cars constructed between 1930 and 1940. Three different manufacturers (American Car and Foundry, Pullman-Standard, and Pressed Steel) were used. #1281 is representative of this fleet, usually called the R1-9 series because the contract numbers began with R1 and ended with R9. Pullman-Standard built this car in 1936 as part of the R6 contract. NYTM

IND R1-9 car at the 1939–1940 World's Fair Station, served by trains from the Queens Boulevard Line that used tracks that provide access to and from the Jamaica Yard. The absence of people is most likely because this photo is a test train shortly before the April 1939 opening. The service was not replicated for the 1964–1965 World's Fair. NYTM

way that closed when the fair did, charged ten cents for a trip to the fair before and after unification, unlike the standard nickel tariff on the IRT-BMT combined service on the Flushing Line. On the IND, an extra nickel was collected from exiting passengers; entering passengers paid ten cents. One of unification's selling points was that it would retain the nickel fare, yet on the city's own new showcase subway to the fair site, a double fare was charged. That too was a glimpse into the future: the subway fare would become ten cents in 1948.

2

1941: A Strike and a Pioneering Labor Agreement

Fifth Avenue Coach Company, whose former routes today form the backbone of New York City Transit's Manhattan Bus Division, started in 1885, using horse-drawn coaches on its namesake avenue. When the twentieth century dawned, the high costs and slow speeds of animal power led its management to search for an alternative, nonrail mode, which turned out to be the new-fangled, gasoline-powered, double-deck motor buses that first appeared in 1907, the first example of an urban mass transit self-propelled bus in North America. Copied after the two-level buses in London, the service was soon so popular that it became a sightseeing attraction despite the fact that its fare was twice the normal five-cent tariff found on its competitors' lines. In the mid-1920s Fifth Avenue Coach acquired control of New York Railways (NYR), which operated most of Manhattan's conduit-powered streetcars.[1] In an eighteen-month period in 1935–1936, the new Fifth Avenue subsidiary New York Omnibus Corporation replaced the entire NYR system with over seven hundred new single-deck buses. With this changeover, the vast majority of Manhattan's surface lines were in the hands of these two affiliated companies.[2] The buses had similar green and cream paint schemes, and the slogan "Go the Motor Coach Way" appeared on both company's vehicles. The Omnibus Corporation, a holding company, owned both firms as well as the Chicago Motor Coach Company, a similar operation in that city.

After 1936, the only remaining streetcar operator in Manhattan was the Third Avenue Railway System, a large conglomerate that also controlled all surface rail and bus operations in the Bronx and a significant network in Westchester County. Third Avenue's bus operations were known as the Surface Transportation System, a firm that itself would later become intertwined with Fifth Avenue Coach. Its Manhattan streetcar routes included Third Avenue, Broadway, Amsterdam Avenue above 125th Street, and

1. A New York City ordinance from about 1890 prohibited Manhattan streetcars from using conventional overhead wires. Instead, power was delivered using a collection shoe (called a plow) that touched an underground third rail through a slot between the two running rails. The only other U.S. city with such a system was Washington, D.C.

2. In addition, two small affiliated bus companies operated crosstown routes on Chambers-Madison Streets, 49th-50th Streets, and 65th Street, plus north-south routes on York, First, and Second Avenues. Third Avenue Railway System still operated a significant streetcar network.

In 1942 on Fifth Avenue in front of the 42nd Street Library, three types of Fifth Avenue Coach double deckers are visible. There is an open-top front engine, a closed-top front engine, and three of the newer "Queen Mary" closed-top buses with rear engines. Motor Bus Society

Taken about 1948 on Queens Boulevard in Elmhurst, this bus is a 1938 single-deck General Motors vehicle that was used on the short #16 Elmhurst Crosstown route and also on the 57th and 72nd Street crosstown routes in Manhattan. Motor Bus Society

Two Queen Mary double-deckers, both model 735s, southbound on Fifth Avenue at 42nd Street, in 1937. Motor Bus Society

crosstown lines on 42nd, 59th, and 125th Streets. Many of its Bronx streetcars connected to Upper Manhattan using the numerous Harlem River bridges.

The question that all this raises is: why were two interlocked companies operating side-by-side, on parallel avenues, charging different fares, instead of just one company? Fifth Avenue Coach charged ten cents, primarily used double-deck buses that required a two-man crew (driver and conductor), and guaranteed a seat to all patrons. In those non–health conscious days, smoking was even permitted on the buses' top decks. Its routes were centered on its namesake avenue and then radiated northward to Harlem and Washington Heights and eastward to Jackson Heights, Queens. As a result the routes were marketed as long-haul, high-class routes; the typical customer's journey was six miles. Fifth Avenue Coach distributed route maps that highlighted points of interest that tourists could easily visit by using its bus network.

By contrast, New York City Omnibus routes were short-haul, urban transit routes that charged the standard five-cent fare found throughout the city, used single-deck,

Fifth Avenue Coach had its own fleet of snow plows. This one is shown southbound on Riverside Drive, probably about 1930. Motor Bus Society

It's 1936, and a brand-new NYCO Yellow model 718 is shown on route #4 on Lexington Avenue at Bloomingdale's, followed by a FACO double-decker on route #15 that has just crossed the Queensboro Bridge. Motor Bus Society

#913 is a 1941 Yellow 4502 model loading passengers for an uptown trip on route #10, about 1942. The blacked-out headlights were required during World War II. Motor Bus Society

Two Fifth Avenue Coach double-deckers, both front-engine models, one with an open top and one with a closed top. Taken at 167th Street and Broadway, early 1940s. Motor Bus Society

one-man buses, and operated on a grid system on most of Manhattan's north-south avenues and important crosstown streets from Delancey to 116th.

Despite the intracorporate competition on the long north-south avenue routes, the nickel-fare lines were financially more successful than their dime-fare brethren. Typical New York City Omnibus customers traveled for just over a mile per trip, creating heavy short-haul, on-off traffic that was constantly turning over seats to new riders, versus the guaranteed seat and scenic riding characteristics on Fifth Avenue routes. Whatever the case, the combined FACO-NYCO network controlled the great majority of Manhattan's surface routes, and its financial successes were noted by the nascent labor organizations that were trying to organize New York's transit workers in the mid-1930s.

This chapter's photos show Fifth Avenue Coach and New York City Omnibus vehicles primarily between 1936 and 1941, when both firms began operating modern rear-engine buses and saw their workers organize into labor unions.

During the mid-1930s, President Roosevelt's New Deal included legislation (the Wagner Act, formally the National Labor Relations Act) that facilitated workers' ability to organize into industrywide labor unions. Prior to the New Deal, transit workers had tried to organize based on individual crafts, much like railroad workers were organized, but they were generally unsuccessful. One reason was that higher-status occupations such as motormen tended to look down on lower-status crafts such as station cleaners. Another reason was that the company managements of all New York transit properties were antiunion. The low wages and poor working conditions of the early 1930s, exacerbated by the Great Depression, made New York transit a fertile field for the new industrial union movement.[3]

The Transport Workers Union (TWU), part of the Congress of Industrial Organizations (CIO), was created in 1934 initially to organize workers on New York's two privately owned subway companies, the IRT and BMT. The TWU also looked to organize workers on the large bus and streetcar companies, notably the Fifth Avenue–New York City Omnibus companies and the Third Avenue Railway System conglomerate that controlled bus and streetcar lines in the Bronx and Manhattan. After protracted and often bitter efforts, in the summer of 1937 the TWU won the right to represent Fifth Avenue's and New York City Omnibus's drivers, conductors, and repair and maintenance workers. The contract required a closed shop—that is, any person hired into a represented job on Fifth Avenue and New York City Omnibus was required to join the TWU as a condition of employment. Third Avenue Railway, which operated the entire bus and trolley system in the Bronx and some Manhattan routes as well, also signed representation agreements with the TWU in 1937.

For over thirty years, the TWU's leader was Michael Quill, an Irish immigrant whose rough-and-tumble public persona was balanced by his reputation behind closed doors as an honest negotiator respected by both his membership and the managements of the transit organizations he unionized. As the labor historian Joshua Freeman has noted, after 1954 "TWU bargaining with the TA became highly stereotyped. . . . Out of public sight, Quill and [Mayor Robert] Wagner would quietly work out an agreement."[4] As will be seen in subsequent chapters, Quill's influence is felt even today, long after his 1966 death.

An article in *Fortune*'s July 1940 issue focused on the three urban bus properties that the Omnibus Corporation owned—Fifth Avenue Coach, New York City Omnibus, and

3. See Joshua Freeman, *In Transit* (New York: Oxford University Press, 1989), chaps. 1 and 2, for a detailed description of the New York transit industry and its workforce up to the mid-1930s.

4. Ibid., 327.

New York Times,
March 11, 1941.

New York Times: (left) March 11, 1941, (right) March 11, 1941.

Chicago Motor Coach.[5] It was noted that management at the two New York bus companies was not happy about seeing its workers come under TWU representation. This was in contrast to its corporate cousin Chicago Motor Coach, where Omnibus Corporation's president John Ritchie managed to keep the workers in a company union, the Motor Coach Employees Fraternity, until the 1940s. Benefits included free medical care, $21 per week sick pay, and interest-free loans up to $50. The difference was that under TWU representation, Fifth Avenue's drivers and conductors enjoyed substantial wage increases and two weeks of vacation with pay.

The same *Fortune* article noted that of the three companies, New York City Omnibus was the big money maker in 1939, with a net profit of $1.9 million. Fifth Avenue Coach was described as a "patrician that has come upon evil days," with a $90,000 loss from its operations the same year, although the article noted that intercompany investments gained it a net profit of $214,000. Fifth Avenue's difficulties were traced to its two-man operation and the company's need to maintain an obsolete fleet of open-top double deckers alongside its more modern closed-top Yellow 720s and 735s, which went into service in 1936–1938. It was also noted that the Great Depression cut into the market of customers who would pay a dime for a guaranteed seat with a view versus the nickel fare on parallel transit lines.

In March 1941 the TWU went on strike against Fifth Avenue Coach and New York City Omnibus, the first major strike against any New York transit property since the

5. *Fortune* (July 1940): 61–67, 92–100.

March 10, 1941, strike notice, distributed when the Transport Workers Union struck NYCO and FACO for a ten-day period. TWU Local 100 archives

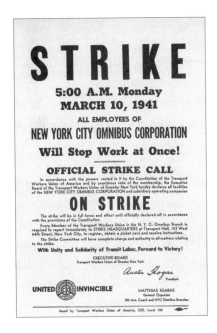

TWU's formation in 1934. The contract between the bus companies and the TWU expired on February 28. After days of fruitless negotiations, the strike began March 10, one day after a major late winter storm dropped a foot of wet snow on the city. The primary issues were wages and benefits—the TWU wanted a 25 percent wage increase, three weeks of paid vacations instead of two, and a uniform eight-hour day. Wages at the time were 90 cents per hour for New York City Omnibus drivers, 81 cents for Fifth Avenue drivers, and 74 cents for Fifth Avenue conductors. Company management offered to submit the dispute to arbitration, but the TWU refused. Charges and countercharges were publicized in the newspapers.

The strike lasted until March 21, left many Manhattan streets and avenues without bus service, and was a major inconvenience to the nine hundred thousand riders affected. While there were some unaffected parallel bus and streetcar routes, and of course subway and elevated lines, the situation was difficult. On March 19 Mayor LaGuardia appointed a three-man fact-finding panel to "formulate and make public the issues in the bus strike that ought to be submitted to arbitration."[6] The strike ended on March 21 when both sides signed an agreement, brokered by the mayor's panel, to submit all issues to arbitration with a stipulation that the new contract would be retroactive to March 1 and at the very least retain the wage and benefit levels of the expired contract. Part of the deal was that the annual operating cost increases under the new contract would be capped at $250,000 for Fifth Avenue Coach and $750,000 for New York City Omnibus. The public perception was that the settlement was more favorable to the TWU. After a day in which garage and shop workers readied the buses for the road, service resumed on March 22.

The panel did not reach its conclusions until July 16, 1941, and granted the workers pay increases ranging from two to eight cents per hour, far less than the 25 percent original demand. Working hours were also improved; Fifth Avenue workers won a basic nine-hour day; New York City Omnibus workers received a basic eight-hour day with time and one-half for work in excess of eight hours.

6. *New York Times* (March 20, 1941).

Immediately after the TWU members went back to work, a new labor issue came to a head. Fifth Avenue and New York City Omnibus maintained four major garage facilities in Manhattan north of 96th Street—100th Street and Lexington Avenue, 102nd Street and Madison Avenue, 146th Street and Lenox Avenue, and 132nd Street and Broadway, the latter also being the corporate headquarters for both companies. Besides this large real estate presence in Harlem and its periphery, Fifth Avenue and New York City Omnibus provided the majority of Upper Manhattan's bus service. Black employees of the two firms were restricted to bus cleaners and washers—none were drivers or mechanics, skilled crafts that commanded higher pay. As a result most black New Yorkers intensely disliked both companies. Harlem community and labor leaders, led by a young Reverend Adam Clayton Powell Jr., organized a boycott of the two companies' routes in order to force the hiring of black drivers and mechanics. Those leaders formed the United Negro Bus Strike Committee to coordinate the boycott and work to break the employment barriers for black drivers and mechanics. The boycott was effective, lasting nearly a month, and reduced the Harlem ridership on both companies' routes. After some incidents, including the throwing of rocks and bottles at some buses, an agreement was reached and signed on April 19, 1941, ending the boycott and beginning a process under which both companies would hire black drivers and mechanics. The *New York Times* headline on April 20 noted, "2 Bus Lines Agree to Employ Negroes."[7]

New York Times, April 20, 1941.

The TWU, while it did not instigate the issue, helped broker the settlement. It was a unique three-party agreement, almost radical for its time, which bore signatures of Fifth Avenue Coach/New York City Omnibus management, the TWU, and the United Negro Bus Strike Committee. It was agreed that after ninety-one furloughed drivers were reemployed, the next hundred driver openings would be reserved for black workers. In the

7. *New York Times* (April 20, 1941).

maintenance area, the next seventy openings would be similarly reserved. After those goals were reached, black and white employees would be hired alternatively until 17 percent of the two companies' drivers and mechanics were black, which represented the black percentage of Manhattan's 1941 population. This was a major initiative and solidified the TWU's reputation as an early advocate of equal employment opportunity.

The first black drivers began working in February 1942, on the #10 Eighth Avenue–Central Park West route.[8] What no one realized at the time was that this agreement foresaw the time when, fifty years later, African American transit workers would be the TWU's top leadership, supplanting the union's traditional Irish hierarchy.

New York Times Times Magazine, January 7, 1949.

On January 9, 1949 the *New York Times Magazine* published an article, "Cold War on the Buses," detailing with some humor the daily problems on New York buses.[9] The article's subtitle was, "Those odd pennies have intensified the feud between hurried passenger and harried driver," meaning that in 1948 fare increases created tariffs of either seven or eleven cents, requiring pennies and slowing boarding and making change. New York City's Franchise Bureau had the power to grant fare increases, but it typically kept increases to a minimum to assuage the public. So when the historic nickel barrier was broken in 1948, the bus companies were granted two increases—to six cents in September and seven cents in December. Fifth Avenue Coach routes, which had been ten cents from its inception, got a penny increase in 1948, which in turn would go up to twelve cents in late 1949. The odd-penny fares made making change cumbersome and forced passengers to deposit pennies and nickels or dimes into two separate fareboxes.

While the article noted that "85 to 90 percent of the drivers for the two largest private companies [Surface Transportation System and Fifth Avenue/New York City Om-

8. *New York Times* (February 1, 1942).
9. *New York Times Magazine* (January 7, 1949).

146th Street and Lenox Avenue NYCO depot, in about 1948. The depot is still in use today but has been renamed Mother Hale Depot. Yellow 740 #431 and GM 4507 #1871 let us compare pre- and postwar bus models, respectively. Motor Bus Society

nibus] are of Irish descent," the writer also duly cited the 1941 Fifth Avenue Coach agreement to hire black drivers ("In 1941 one big company began hiring Negroes") and said that there were about four hundred African American bus drivers in New York in 1949—no doubt thanks to the pioneering 1941 agreement. The *Times* article also noted that "the average New York bus driver is a loyal union man. The TWU 'got the vote' in 1937 and has gained for him a security and a living standard which he is determined to keep."

1941: Dyre Avenue Subway Extension Opens

3

Looking at today's subway map, the #5 Lexington Avenue subway spur between East 180th Street and Dyre Avenue in the northeastern Bronx looks like just another branch of the huge New York City subway system. A look back into history will reveal that it is unlike any other subway route. Trains began rolling on the #5 line's tracks in 1912, but not as part of the New York subway. When the line was new, it was part of the New York, Westchester, and Boston Railroad (NYWB), a heavy-duty commuter rail route designed to connect a number of southern Westchester County communities (such as New Rochelle, Larchmont, Mamaroneck, White Plains, and Port Chester) with subway and elevated trains in the Bronx. Despite its name, the NYWB never came near Boston. It was a subsidiary of the larger New York, New Haven, and Hartford Railroad (more commonly known as the New Haven Railroad), which dominated rail transportation in southern New England and was the main rail link between New York and Boston.

The NYWB was built to handle passenger capacities that never materialized. It was four tracks wide on its Bronx portion between East 133rd Street and Dyre Avenue, after which it continued into Westchester on a pair of double-track branches. Its rolling stock was state-of-the-art electric multiple-unit cars that combined the best features of railroad and subway equipment, and its stations were set up for off-train, rapid-transit-style fare collection. Unfortunately, the NYWB's fatal flaw was its South Bronx terminus at East 133rd Street, which forced its customers to transfer to IRT subway and elevated trains to continue their trips to mid-Manhattan, versus taking the parent New Haven Railroad's trains directly between the same Lower Westchester communities and Grand Central Terminal. The NYWB route cost less than the New Haven but could not compete with the parent company's direct, one-seat ride between the Westchester suburbs and mid-Manhattan. Passengers who had a choice complained about the higher fare in and out of Grand Central, but not enough of them rode the NYWB to allow it to turn a profit. This intrafamily competition proved a continuing drain on parent New Haven's finances, as the New Haven was responsible for paying interest and amortization on the NYWBs bonds that weren't covered from fares.[1]

1. Stan Fischler, *The Subway* (New York: H&M Productions, 1997), 174–180.

New York Westchester and Boston Railway (NYWB) just south of its East 180th Street station, probably in the 1920s. Note the four tracks, overhead power supply, and well-ballasted right of way. IRT cars laid up outside its East 180th Street barn are on the left. At the time no one could foresee the union of the two routes. NYTM

East 180th Street Station viewed from the east (Morris Park Avenue) side, just before the NYWB closed in 1937. NYC Transit still uses the imposing building today. NYTM

It's now 1941, and at Baychester Avenue the NYC transit system is operating this two-car train of former IRT elevated cars. The new third rail is on the two outside tracks; overhead wires and middle tracks were no longer needed. NYTM

Dyre Avenue train passing over a newly widened Boston Road, between the Dyre and Baychester stations. Sparse vehicle traffic suggests that this photo was taken during World War II. NYTM

The Depression of the 1930s hurt both railroads. The New Haven entered bankruptcy in 1935, and the NYWB immediately followed its parent on the same path. Unable to make the bond payments to the NYWB's creditors, the New Haven officially terminated service on the NYWB as of December 31, 1937, and moved to liquidate its entire property in the Bronx and Westchester.

As the saying goes, "timing is everything." In the late 1930s, New York City was contemplating an extension of the new IND Concourse subway (opened in July 1933) beyond its northern terminal at East 205th Street and Bainbridge Avenue. In May 1939 the *New York Times* reported that the Bronx Board of Trade urged the Board of Transportation to extend the IND subway northeast along Burke Avenue. This proposal was originally a small part of the Second Phase of the IND system, a large list of subway expansion projects proposed in the late 1920s but never built. One such proposal extended the Concourse IND subway from 205th Street along Burke Avenue and Boston Road to Baychester Avenue, including a transfer to the IRT White Plains Road line at Burke Avenue. The 1929 stock market crash and the subsequent Great Depression killed the IND's Second Phase, but the need for additional rapid transit in the far northeast corner of the Bronx was still recognized. With the NYWB right-of-way now available and unused, in January 1940 the Board of Transportation acquired the NYWB right-of-way within the Bronx, between East 180th Street and Dyre Avenue, for $1,875,000. An additional million dollars was spent to install a third rail system and old BMT elevated signals, modify platforms for IRT cars, and rehabilitate twenty old Manhattan elevated cars for the service. The five former NYWB stations at Morris Park, Pelham Parkway, Gun Hill Road, Baychester Avenue, and Dyre Avenue were modified for turnstile fare collection, and the new extension opened on May 15, 1941.

New York Times, May 16, 1941.

Dubbed the Dyre Avenue Line, it was shown on subway maps as part of the IRT division, branching from the White Plains Road line at East 180th Street. It began at the old NYWB headquarters building at East 180th Street and Morris Park Avenue and continued northward, stopping at the railroad's old stations—Morris Park, Pelham Parkway, Gun Hill Road, Baychester Avenue, and Dyre Avenue, a short distance south of the Bronx-Westchester boundary. No revenue track connections were built at East 180th Street to the IRT White Plains Road line; customers walked the short distance between the Dyre Avenue and White Plains Road Line stations, right through the lobby of the ex-NYWB headquarters. Originally the Board of Transportation was planning to charge riders an extra nickel for Dyre Avenue service, but political expediency, and the fact that the nearby White Plains Road Line also reached to the Westchester border, induced the Board of Transportation to create a free transfer at East 180th Street so that

Gun Hill Road Station in 1947. Overhead wire, support gantries, and two middle tracks have been removed. NYTM

Baychester Avenue Station, 1947, showing an area with much vacant land. NYTM

It's 1954, and a two-car shuttle train of IRT deck roof equipment is approaching East 180th Street from the north. In about three years this scene will change as the connection between the Dyre and White Plains Road lines will be completed and put into daily operation. NYTM

Street-level station building at Gun Hill Road in 1947. Notice the sign saying "south bound to East 180th St. and IRT Division." That was a subtle way of saying that the Dyre Avenue Line was, in those days, part of the IND division, although the riding public didn't know and didn't care. NYTM

Dyre Avenue passengers, while still required to change trains, could at least ride for the same nickel all over the city.

The day of the opening ceremony Mayor Stanley Church of New Rochelle, immediately north of the Dyre Avenue terminal, suggested extending the subway service into his municipality. Mayor LaGuardia was polite but turned down the request, saying, "I have all I can do to clean the streets of New York City and I can't run Westchester."[2] Lost to history is the fact that even though the Dyre Avenue Line looked like an IRT route (a blue line) on the official subway maps and used old IRT elevated equipment, it was actually and officially a part of the IND Division of the Board of Transporta-

2. *New York Times* (May 16, 1941).

tion. Its motormen and conductors were on the IND seniority lists. To the daily rider, this made no difference, of course, but it is one of those historical tidbits forgotten today.

Another even more obscure historical footnote dates from right after the line's original abandonment. As reported in the *New York Times* on February 6, 1938, Robert Moses, then New York City's parks commissioner and highway construction czar, proposed converting the NYWB right-of-way between 174th Street (the Bronx) and Port Chester into a trucks-only toll highway, to relieve traffic on the parallel Boston Post Road (U.S. Highway 1).[3] The Moses truck highway proposal was attacked immediately and died a quick death. In 1958 the New England Thruway in the Bronx and Westchester, as well as the connecting Connecticut Turnpike, both parts of Interstate 95, were opened, traversing the same travel corridor. Moses, of course, was the driving force behind the New England Thruway,[4] but his aborted proposal to build a truckway on the old NYWB roadbed was one of the few times that one of his road-building ideas was thwarted and never again resurrected.

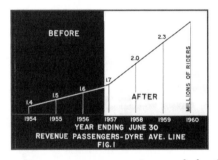

Graph showing how Dyre Avenue Line revenue passengers increased after through-train service was instituted in May 1957, as published in the NYC Transit Authority Annual Report for Year Ending June 30, 1960. NYTM

When originally opened, the Dyre Avenue Line used two-car, wooden trains rescued from the Second and Ninth Avenue elevateds when those routes were abandoned. In the early 1950s older steel subway cars replaced the original rolling stock. In those days, the Dyre Avenue route was unique for reasons other than its hybrid IND-IRT oversight. Its stations were manned only for one shift, after which train conductors collected fares on board using bus-type fare boxes. Between 1 AM and 5:30 AM the line was completely shut down, unique among New York subway routes.

The big change came in 1957, upon completion of a $3,000,000 track connection north of East 180th Street that permitted through-train service between the IRT Lexington Avenue and Seventh Avenue subways and the Dyre Avenue branch. Additional work included new signal and power supply systems to enable full-length subway trains

3. *New York Times* (February 6, 1938).
4. Robert Caro, *The Power Broker* (New York: Knopf, 1974), 838.

Old IRT elevated cars stored on the Dyre Avenue Line viaduct at East 180th Street, about 1952. An advertising sign visible just below the viaduct advertises the Macy's branch in Parkchester, about two miles from this location. NYTM

In pre-Metrocard times after 9 PM, the Dyre Avenue Line token booths were unmanned, and fares were collected on board the trains by equipping the cars with bus-type fare boxes. Conductors made change for the riders. This photo dates from the mid-1950s, when smoking was fashionable and young boys rode happily around the Bronx. NYTM

Fan trip on then-new R29 cars in 1962, arriving at the Dyre Avenue Station, then a single track. NYTM

Morris Park Station in the mid-1950s, showing the handsome Spanish Mission–style architecture the NYW&B used. This building is thankfully preserved today. NYTM

Pelham Parkway Station in early 1960s as fluorescent lighting is being installed. The NYW&B Railroad built this station below ground in order to follow the ground contour in the area, making it the only "subway" station on the Dyre Avenue Line. NYTM

to operate. Beginning on May 4, 1957, Seventh Avenue express trains (today's #2 train) began operating between East 180th Street and Dyre Avenue, permitting the old NYWB station platforms at East 180th to close. In 1965 the Lexington Avenue #5 express became the Dyre Avenue branch service when the #2 train was shifted full time to the White Plains Road–East 241st Street branch. Today the #5 still performs that function.

4

1941–1948: Third Avenue Transit

RAILS TO RUBBER

In August 1948 the Third Avenue Transit System, the successor to the Third Avenue Railway Company, replaced its last New York City streetcars with diesel buses, ending nearly a century of rail-based street transit in Manhattan and the Bronx. The firm's management and New York City's government were both enthusiastic about the conversion, which was expected to improve the company's operations with a fleet of modern buses. In reality, the conversions created new sets of issues that catapulted Third Avenue Transit into bankruptcy and led to its eventual takeover by Fifth Avenue Coach Company.

As urban transit history goes, Third Avenue's travails were unique and interesting. One example stems from the name itself. The company began as the Third Avenue Railway in 1853, operating a horsecar line on Manhattan's Third Avenue between City Hall and Harlem. Seventy-plus years later, in 1924, Third Avenue controlled a huge streetcar network that encompassed Manhattan, the Bronx, and Westchester County. In that year it formed a subsidiary with the generic-sounding name Surface Transportation Corporation of New York to put itself in position to expand its route network using buses to serve then-undeveloped Bronx neighborhoods without the expense of track and electrical systems needed for streetcars. In 1928, New York City awarded Surface Transportation franchises for twelve new Bronx bus routes.[1] In 1942 the parent company, recognizing that its streetcars were entering their final years, changed its name to Third Avenue Transit System.

Third Avenue was always in the forefront of new technology. Manhattan's tremendous northward growth after 1880 made horsecars unsatisfactory. In 1885 the initial Third Avenue–125th Street route was extended northward along Amsterdam Avenue above 125th Street, using newly developed cable power, by which the cars were propelled using an underground cable between the two running rails. By 1893 cable power was extended to cover the entire route from City Hall to Washington Heights.[2] By then electric streetcars had been perfected, but this new technological breakthrough was initially not permitted in Manhattan because city ordinances forbade overhead wires after the devastating March 1888 blizzard. Third Avenue developed an underground

---

1. Frederick A. Kramer, *Third Avenue Railway* (Flanders, N.J.: RAE, 2001), 4.
2. Ibid., 4.

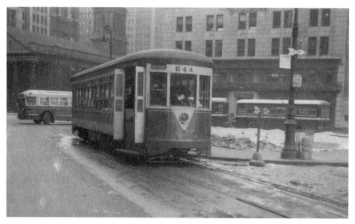

Taken at Park Row and Broadway about 1945 on a gloppy winter day, this photo shows three different private companies' vehicles. Most prominent is Third Avenue Railway System (TARS) streetcar #644, about to begin its twelve-mile northbound run on the company's flagship route, which stretched from this point to 190th Street and Amsterdam Avenue. Converted to bus in May 1947, it remains alive and well in the twenty-first century as bus routes M101 and M103.

The bus turning left behind #644 is NYC Omnibus Yellow Coach model 740 on the #1 Madison Avenue route, which was Manhattan's first major rail-to-bus conversion in 1935. The two smaller buses to the left, Mack CMs operating on the M13 First Avenue route, are part of the small East Side Omnibus Corporation, taken over by the NYC Board of Transportation in 1948.

The building behind the NYC Omnibus is St. Paul's chapel, which achieved lasting fame on September 11, 2001, when it survived the terrorist attacks on the World Trade Center, which was located immediately to its west. NYTM

conduit system for its cars using a third rail buried in a slot that was adapted from cable car technology. A device under each streetcar, a plow, connected the car to its power supply, similar to a subway third rail shoe pointed down instead of left or right. While this system eliminated all overhead wires, it was very expensive to build and maintain. Washington, D.C., was the only other U.S. city to use a streetcar conduit system.

In 1898 Third Avenue took control of the Union Railway, which operated streetcar lines in the Bronx and southern Westchester County, so by 1900 the firm controlled routes from New York's City Hall as far north as Westchester's county seat in White Plains. This network included all Bronx lines and Manhattan-based routes beyond the flagship Third Avenue–125th Street–Amsterdam Avenue route; specifically Broadway–42nd Street, Broadway–Kingsbridge, Tenth Avenue, and crosstown routes on 42nd, 59th, and 125th Streets. North of 125th Street, many Third Avenue routes connected the Bronx and Upper Manhattan using the many Harlem River bridges. In the Bronx, trolley wire was permitted, but routes between the two boroughs at three locations—125th, 135th, and 145th Streets—had to switch from one type of power to the other on the Manhattan side of the Harlem River at a plow pit, an underground vault located in the middle of the tracks just below the surface. A pit man was stationed at these three locations in order to disconnect one type of power and connect the other one. A few low-volume routes in

Lower Manhattan were powered by storage battery cars to avoid the conduit system's high construction costs, but Third Avenue stopped running such cars by 1932.

During the two decades from 1910 until 1930, the Bronx experienced a huge population growth, from 430,980 to 1,265,258, nearly a threefold increase. Massive subway expansions during this period were largely responsible for the dense residential neighborhoods that became synonymous with the Bronx and also created a secondary market for local surface routes as well. Third Avenue's streetcar routes were the primarily supplier to this market, but as population expanded into the borough's developing far northern and eastern sections, buses were seen as a more economical means to provide transit because expensive track and wire construction would not be needed. In the 1920s, the New York City government recognized that the bus was here to stay as a mass transit vehicle, thanks to its relatively quick response to new populations and the resulting transportation demands. The city government assumed direct control over the franchises granted for bus routes.

Seeing this trend, Third Avenue Railway created a bus subsidiary in 1924, Surface Transportation System, for the purpose of expanding bus operations in the Bronx. The same year Manhattan's Fifth Avenue Coach Company expanded operations beyond its namesake avenue and created two bus routes in the Bronx, both on the Grand Concourse. These routes lasted only until 1928, when New York City granted Surface Transportation System an exclusive Bronx bus franchise; both were transferred to Surface Transportation and became routes BX1 and BX2 (Concourse–138th St. and Concourse–Hub respectively). Today under New York City Transit both are still operated largely on their original routings. This franchise award began a series of events that would culminate, twenty years later, in the complete replacement of Third Avenue's Manhattan and Bronx streetcar routes to buses.

Third Avenue did not stop with the Concourse routes and soon established bus routes on Prospect Avenue, Bainbridge Avenue, Eastern (later Bruckner) Boulevard, Boston Road, Williamsbridge Road, Eastchester Road, 170th Street, Pelham Parkway, Castle Hill Avenue, and Gun Hill Road. In the late 1930s Third Avenue began using diesel-powered buses, including a series of dual-powered vehicles that used diesel engines to drive electric generators that in turn powered electric motors for propulsion. While the company did not participate in the development of the newer streamlined PCC cars in the early 1930s,[3] its own shops manufactured a number of lightweight streetcars at the same time in order to provide reliable service on its rail network; some secondhand cars purchased from transit firms outside New York were also rebuilt for continued use on Third Avenue routes. While this was going on, Third Avenue's bus

3. The PCC (President's Conference Committee) car was a streamlined streetcar developed in the early 1930s that operated in Brooklyn from 1936 to 1956 but never anywhere else in New York City. Chapter 1 provides more details about PCC cars.

Third Avenue car #188 on Amsterdam Avenue at 128th Street, in May 1947, close to the last day this line operated streetcars. GMC buses, including the two in the photo, would take over. The company's Amsterdam streetcar depot is on the right, a block north. NYTM

A block north of the Amsterdam depot, the last day of streetcar operation, May 17, 1947. A new GMC bus on the left is no doubt impatiently waiting to receive its passengers, which will happen tomorrow. NYTM

Broadway at West 104th Street, looking north, on December 3, 1946, two weeks before the last streetcar ran on this route. Stanley's Cafeteria on the right was a neighborhood landmark until the early 1970s. The author's first home was two blocks away. NYTM

A block away, Broadway at West 105th Street, this time looking south on August 18, 1947, showing one of the GMC buses that replaced the streetcars. The subway improvement sign refers to the platform lengthening project then underway at the IRT's 103rd Street Station. NYTM

drivers, streetcar operators, and shop forces came under union representation (Transport Workers Union) in 1937, the same year that Fifth Avenue Coach and New York City Omnibus signed labor agreements with the TWU.

So it was in the late 1930s, as the company's franchises were about to expire, that Mayor Fiorello LaGuardia made it clear that his vision of a modern New York did not include streetcars.[4] The 1935–1936 conversion of the New York Railways network in Manhattan convinced his administration that the bus was the long-term future of all surface lines in the five boroughs. In Third Avenue's case, the city used the leverage of its franchise powers to convince the company to convert its rail lines to bus if it wanted

4. Kramer, *Third Avenue Railway*, 4.

to keep its system in operation. Company management, under the leadership of President Slaughter Huff,[5] was similarly convinced that buses were its future. The elimination of tracks, overhead wires, and underground conduits meant the end of costly maintenance. Buses could make curbside stops and were flexible in mixed street traffic. These arguments were too great for streetcar partisans to counter. Accordingly, Third Avenue signed a twenty-five-year franchise agreement in 1940 that promised full bus conversion of all routes by 1960.

As reported in the *New York Times*,[6] on August 21, 1939, Mayor LaGuardia, appearing at World's Fair City Hall, announced his grand plan to motorize the entire Third Avenue Railway streetcar network in Manhattan and the Bronx. Under the plan the 42nd Street crosstown and Broadway lines would be converted as soon as possible, followed by the remaining routes in both boroughs. The mayor was quoted that "this plan provides for a complete substitution of modern, up-to-date buses, during a period of years, on all trolley lines of the Third Avenue system within the City of New York."

No time was lost beginning the conversion. Orders for three hundred new buses were placed with Twin Coach, Yellow Coach (a part of General Motors and after 1943 GM's Coach Division), and Mack Truck. In January 1941 the Morris Avenue streetcar was the first to go bus, followed by the long and heavily used Willis Avenue–125th Street line in August. In the latter case the bus conversion was hastened by the city's decision to convert the adjacent Willis Avenue and Third Avenue Bridges over the Harlem River to a one-way couplet operation, requiring the removal of streetcar tracks. Additional conversions were planned for Manhattan in 1942, beginning with the 59th Street crosstown line.

Only 115 of the buses were delivered before the United States' entry into World War II on December 7, 1941, put an end to the bus conversions, as fossil fuels and rubber tires became scarce for nonmilitary uses. The U.S. government bought the remaining 185 buses in Third Avenue's order and assigned the vehicles to work at a number of Navy facilities, carrying military personnel. Accordingly, the Third Avenue system remained predominantly streetcar operated until after hostilities ended and the civilian production of buses, fuels, and tires could resume. In 1942 the company officially changed its name to Third Avenue Transit Corporation, reflecting the eventual conversion to all-bus operations.

5. Slaughter Huff was a long-time transit executive who was Third Avenue Railway's president from 1918 until 1945. He also was an executive of two Brooklyn streetcar operators from 1908 until 1918, including a stint at the Brooklyn Rapid Transit Company. He is probably best remembered for overseeing Third Avenue's in-house construction of seventy-five double-ended streetcars, dubbed "Huffliners," that served the Manhattan conduit-powered routes until 1947. He died at the age of eighty at his Carmel, New York, home on October 16, 1947.

6. *New York Times* (August 22, 1939).

In 1946, with the war over and civilian bus production once again possible, Third Avenue decided to accelerate bus conversions, starting with the Manhattan routes. In November and December, the 59th, 42nd, Tenth Avenue, and Broadway–42nd routes were motorized; in May and June 1947 respectively, the Third–Amsterdam and Broadway–Kingsbridge routes changed over. After June 29, 1947, no more Manhattan-based streetcars operated, although two Bronx-based crosstown routes that entered upper Manhattan hung on until July 11, 1948.

The end of the Broadway–Kingsbridge streetcar was marked with a ceremony that attracted 1,200 people to 125th Street and Seventh Avenue on Saturday afternoon, June 28, 1947. As *The New York Times* reported, a "streamlined" GMC bus, the last Broadway–Kingsbridge car (a mid-1930s rebuilt model), and nineteenth-century horse-drawn car were lined up on the street. Manhattan Borough President Hugo Rogers, Third Avenue Transit President John MacDonald, and the film actress Joan Leslie took part.[7]

New York Times, June 29, 1947.

It took another fourteen months to convert the remaining Bronx rail routes. Starting March 9, 1947, with the Sound View Avenue line, Bronx streetcars departed one by one until the last four routes—Southern Boulevard, Boston Road, Williamsbridge, and Tremont Avenue—were motorized on August 22, 1948, making Third Avenue's New York City operations 100 percent bus. Third Avenue's Westchester lines continued to run until as late as 1950 (New Rochelle) and 1952 (Yonkers). After 1948, the Third Avenue name disappeared from the sides of the vehicles with the end of streetcar opera-

7. *New York Times* (June 29, 1947).

tions; now its buses sported the moniker "Surface Transportation System" and "Ride the Surface Way" on their outsides.

The fast changeover to buses, not required until 1960 under the franchise, opened up a series of problems that would plague Surface Transportation for the rest of its existence. The city's refusal to allow an increase in the five-cent fare until 1948 was the biggest problem but certainly not the only one. The company wanted an eight-cent fare; the City's Bureau of Franchises permitted increases only to six cents (September 1948) and seven cents (December 1948). Postwar inflation caused increases in fuel, maintenance, and labor costs, and the new bus fleet had to be financed by loans from banks and insurance companies. The large force of streetcar operators had to be retrained to drive buses; some lacked driver's licenses. The company management and the TWU frequently clashed over wages and working conditions, and the company's stockholders frequently revolted. The company owed back franchise taxes to New York City, because the other fiscal pressures put a big strain on its cash flow.

The result was a series of management upheavals at Third Avenue Transit that flared up as World War II was winding down. In June 1945 long-time company president Slaughter Huff was ousted in a proxy battle and replaced by Victor McQuistion, who in turn was forced out in May 1947 during another proxy fight. John MacDonald became the new president and was quoted in the *New York Times* on May 16, 1947, that Third Avenue had not paid a common stock dividend in twenty nine years,[8] indicative of the financial constraints it was facing and the reason for the stockholder unrest. In 1948 MacDonald himself yielded the company presidency to James Hodes. These frequent and unscheduled management changes did not help solve Third Avenue's challenges; problems were simply passed from one management team to the next.

In October 1948 a dissident group of the company's bondholders tried to force bankruptcy because of their impatience at the company's inability to solve its financial issues. With the fare and labor issues always in the immediate background, the camel's back finally broke on June 21, 1949, when Third Avenue filed for, and was granted, voluntary bankruptcy protection. The company's counsel, Mortimer Gordon, as reported in the *New York Times* on June 22, stated that the key reason for the bankruptcy request was New York City's refusal to permit an eight-cent fare, which New York State's Public Service Commission had already approved. At the same time, the city was attempting to collect back franchise taxes and was threatening to cancel the company's franchises if it asked for an eight-cent fare. Third Avenue Transit was caught in a classic rock-and-a-hard-place situation. The bankruptcy action protected the company from its creditors, including the city, and permitted it to work out means to pay its bills in an orderly fashion.[9]

8. *New York Times* (May 16, 1947).
9. *New York Times* (June 22, 1949).

Federal Judge Samuel Kaufman, who granted the petition after a sometimes acrimonious day-long hearing, permitted James Hodes to continue as Third Avenue's president. This was despite remarks from the ousted former president, Victor McQuistion, who said during the hearing that it would be "a grave error" if Hodes was allowed to remain at the helm.[10] McQuistion charged that the Hodes team had engaged in mismanagement. Mortimer Gordon, Third Avenue's attorney, retorted that McQuistion had been removed from his presidency in 1947 by court order. Although no one knew it at the time, Third Avenue would remain in receivership until it was absorbed into Fifth Avenue Coach in 1956 (see Chapter 14).

The bus conversions, given the speed at which the company wanted to replace all streetcars, also had issues stemming from the financial problems. In its first postwar bus order Third Avenue specified forty-five-passenger diesel vehicles to convert the Manhattan routes. This order went to General Motors (GM) for two groups of TDH4506 and TDH4507 models, which were its first postwar diesel transit buses and included the hydraulic transmissions developed just before World War II. In 1948, to complete its bus conversion, Third Avenue ordered three hundred more diesels, this time from Mack Truck, whose model C45 had just been added to its product line. Because of the ongoing management and financial issues, only 185 of the three hundred buses were procured; the remaining 115 were bought by New York City's Board of Transportation to equip a group of Manhattan routes that had been taken over from two private operators (Comprehensive Omnibus and East Side Omnibus) in September 1948. Ironically, these two companies sold out to the city because they could not manage with a five-cent fare—the same issue that Surface Transportation was facing at this time (see Chapter 6).

During the postwar period Third Avenue became embroiled in many labor issues that garnered it much media attention over seemingly trivial items. In 1948, when its base fare was raised in two increments from five to seven cents in the midst of the changeover of Bronx routes from streetcar to bus, a problem arose when the odd pennies could not be registered in existing fare boxes. Boarding passengers had to hand one or two cents to the driver after depositing a nickel in the box, and the driver in turn had to place the pennies in a separate receptacle. This was occurring while many of the bus operators had just been converted from working streetcars, where no steering wheel was needed. At the same time the fare was increased, the New York City Board of Transportation raised the subway fare from a nickel to a dime. To reduce the impact on riders who had to use subways and surface vehicles, bus and streetcar riders in boroughs outside Manhattan could purchase a combination fare totaling twelve cents to ride subways and connecting surface routes at designated locations. Passengers boarding buses and streetcars purchased a transfer from the driver, while passengers leaving

10. *New York Times* (June 22, 1949).

the subway purchased a two-cent transfer in the paid area of the station that was good on designated surface routes at that location. In Third Avenue's case, the six-cent fare resulted in its drivers being required to sell a six-cent transfer ticket as well, adding to the stress and frustration of the job. Drivers already had to collect the proper local fare and dispense separate, free paper transfers good on other Third Avenue routes. These duties were in addition to the basic chores of driving in heavy traffic, operating two doors, and making change.

Third Avenue's management and the TWU locked horns over this issue and many others in the late 1940s, during the bus conversion program. Strikes were threatened frequently but did not occur except for short wildcat disputes. Third Avenue was caught between the city's desire to keep fares as low as possible and the TWU's posturing for higher wages and improved working conditions. An issue such as requiring drivers to sell subway transfers was simply another stress that put the company's management between the TWU and the city.

New York Times, April 1, 1947.

It all boiled over when a Bronx driver, William Cimillo, assigned to the BX15 Gun Hill Road route, decided that New York traffic and the job's stresses were too much to handle. One morning in March 1947, Cimillo drove over the George Washington Bridge and did not stop until he reached Hollywood, Florida, where he phoned his bosses to ask them to wire money for fuel so he could return to New York. Charged with grand larceny and escorted back to the Bronx by police, Cimillo's job was saved through the intercession of the TWU and individual acts of his fellow drivers. He was reinstated on probation for a year and continued to drive Bronx buses without incident for many years afterward, even though his episode was not forgotten. A March 1960 article in the *New York Times Magazine* about New York bus drivers noted Cimillo's earlier misdeed but noted that after he returned to the Bronx he "became a national

In the late 1930s Surface Transportation purchased a series of Twin Coach diesel-electric buses to replace its initial fleet. One, #939, is shown on route BX2 southbound on the Grand Concourse around 1940. NYTM

In 1940–1941 Surface purchased a fleet of Mack diesel buses to begin the conversion of its trolley routes. Before World War II stopped the conversions, route BX29/Willis Avenue was equipped with these buses. Two are shown about 1950 at the Fordham Road terminus of the route, with the IRT's Third Avenue El overhead. NYTM

Three photos illustrate the last days of Bronx streetcars, all converted to bus in 1947–1948. The image at the upper-left shows #382, a mid-1930s rebuilt car, at West Farms Square on the Tremont Avenue Line. The bus on the left is a 1947 Twin Coach on route Q44 to Flushing and Jamaica, recently taken over by the NYC Board of Transportation from North Shore Bus. This route was one of the last four Bronx streetcars, becoming a bus on August 22, 1948. The image above shows #1252 on the University Avenue Line near Jerome Park reservoir; this car was part of a group of second-hand units purchased from Staten Island. The Sanitation Department truck on the right is typical of the 1940s-style elevator-type collection vehicles ubiquitous in those days. Finally, the image to the left shows a World War I–era convertible car on the 180th Street crosstown route, on University Avenue just south of Tremont Avenue. NYTM

A GMC 4507 on route BX27/Clason Point, about 1950. Trolley tracks are still in the roadway of Sound View Avenue. This neighborhood did not become built up until the late 1950s. NYTM

Three models of Surface Transportation buses are shown at West Farms Depot, about 1952. Left to right are a prewar Twin Coach, a prewar Yellow (GMC), and a postwar GMC. NYTM

hero."[11] He duly noted that he was never again tempted to go AWOL with his bus, saying that a joke told a second time is not funny.

Thirty-five years after his 1975 death, Cimillo's adventure was once again remembered in the *New York Times*. In August 2010, a Jet Blue flight attendant, Steven Slater, fed up with the stresses of his job at the conclusion of a trip, infamously slid out of his plane via an emergency chute at John F. Kennedy International Airport. An article compared Slater, albeit unfavorably, to Cimillo, who, unlike Slater, retained his job.[12]

Fares went to six cents in September 1948, seven cents in December 1948, and eight cents in August 1949, but the company could not escape the bankruptcy court despite its new bus fleet and the fare increases. Surface Transportation remained in receivership until December 1956, managing to operate and even adding 243 new Mack and GM buses between 1949 and 1953 at the behest of the New York State Public Service Commission, which had jurisdiction over privately owned urban bus companies.

On December 17, 1956, Fifth Avenue Coach Lines formally purchased Surface Transportation, creating what then was the largest privately owned urban bus operation in the United States. The Fifth Avenue–Surface amalgamation would last until 1962, when the New York City took over the operations of both firms after a new management group provoked a sudden strike. These events will be covered in Chapters 14 and 16 respectively.

11. *New York Times Magazine* (March 13, 1960).
12. *New York Times* (August 10, 2010).

5

1944 and 1950: Goodbye to Brooklyn Bridge Rails

Since its 1883 opening, the Brooklyn Bridge has hosted multiple forms of urban transport—pedestrians, bicycles, horse-drawn vehicles, cable cars, electric-powered trolleys and elevateds, motor cars and taxicabs. Since 1950, aside from walkers and cyclists, only the latter two vehicles have been able to cross it. New Yorkers of a longer memory will recall that from 1898 until 1944 the Brooklyn Bridge was a major rail transit route between its namesake borough and Lower Manhattan. Trolleys from numerous routes and elevateds from many branches of Brooklyn's once far-flung system crossed the bridge on parallel tracks and terminated at a large, jointly used, two-story structure opposite City Hall. Known as Park Row Terminal, it was an important gateway to and from Brooklyn for nearly fifty years.

Soon after the bridge opened in May 1883, a cable car line powered by stationary steam engines on both sides of the river provided the first mass transit on the span. Brooklyn was then a separate city, and at the same time began developing steam elevated train routes to serve its growing population. The first such route opened above Lexington Avenue in 1885, and by the early 1890s the fledgling el network expanded to include routes along Myrtle Avenue, Fulton Street, Fifth Avenue/Third Avenue, and Broadway (street names are Brooklyn thoroughfares, which except for Myrtle Avenue have Manhattan counterparts that were not part of this system).

Passengers on Lexington, Myrtle, Fulton, and Fifth Avenue els originally had to transfer to the Brooklyn Bridge cable cars in order to reach Manhattan. Beginning in 1898, with the consolidation of Brooklyn into New York City and the electrification of the bridge's tracks, through trains were operated between many Brooklyn el routes and the Park Row terminal. The elevated lines were converted to electric power beginning in 1899 as well, resulting in the end of cable car shuttle operation in 1908. At the same time, many Brooklyn trolley routes, themselves newly electrified in the early 1890s, were extended to Park Row. Examples were the Smith Street, Fulton Street, DeKalb Avenue, Graham Avenue, Vanderbilt Avenue, and Seventh Avenue lines.

Between the end of the Civil War and 1897, the City of Brooklyn itself expanded its boundaries. Originally limited to areas close to Manhattan, the growing city absorbed suburban and semirural towns and villages in its periphery whose names are today

Brooklyn Bridge at its Brooklyn entrance in 1938, showing private autos, a PCC streetcar, and a BMT el train all heading toward Manhattan. NYTM

Fifth Avenue el at Atlantic and Flatbush Avenues in 1940, shortly before it stopped running. This was one of the lines that crossed the Brooklyn Bridge. NYTM

Fulton Street el train at Vanderbilt Avenue shortly before its 1940 closing. It too crossed the Brooklyn Bridge. NYTM

Fulton el train in downtown Brooklyn in 1940, soon to be closed. NYTM

synonymous with Brooklyn neighborhoods. Flatbush, Flatlands, Gravesend, New Lots, Williamsburgh, and Coney Island are examples of towns and villages that became twentieth-century urban neighborhoods. Beginning around 1870, the latter community developed itself as a summer resort destination for both day trippers from the more settled areas and even for overnight visitors looking for a vacation. The local business magnates of the day saw the potential of railroads connecting Coney Island with the more developed Kings County communities. Beginning in 1864, these businessmen were behind a number of steam railroad lines constructed to connect the City of Brooklyn to Coney Island. The difference between these lines and the elevateds noted above is that the Coney Island routes originally operated mostly at street-grade level through much undeveloped and semirural territory, unlike the elevated, which operated above public streets. These surface steam lines evolved into today's still-familiar names of the Brighton Beach, Culver, West End, and Sea Beach routes. As an example, the name Culver refers to Andrew Culver (1832–1906), the founder of the Prospect Park and Coney Island Railroad. This road opened in July 1875 between Prospect Park (9th Avenue

Atlantic Avenue el station in East New York in the early 1940s. Note the sign for the Fulton–Lexington Avenue train, headed to Park Row. This was one of the last two routes to cross the Brooklyn Bridge. NYTM

El train leaving Brooklyn heading to Park Row in 1941, on either the Lexington or Myrtle routes. NYTM

DeKalb Avenue streetcar about the cross into Manhattan as the first car to use the former Brooklyn Bridge elevated train tracks. NYTM

Intersection of Adams Street and Myrtle Avenue in November 1943, showing the connection between the Myrtle Avenue el and Brooklyn Bridge. This would be severed five months later when the bridge's el trains stopped running. NYTM

Pictured in November 1943, the mezzanine of the BMT Park Row el-trolley terminal in its last year. By then the Myrtle and Lexington routes were the only el lines left there. NYTM

It's now March 24, 1944, nineteen days after the el trains stopped running, and demolition is already well underway. That scrap steel will no doubt help the war effort. NYTM

and 20th Street) and Surf Avenue and West 5th Street. It principally followed Gravesend Avenue, today's McDonald Avenue and F train route. Even today, the F train's electronic signs refer to it as the Culver Local.

By 1900, the original Brooklyn elevateds and the southern Brooklyn steam railroad routes all came under control of the Brooklyn Rapid Transit Company (BRT), as did the borough's far-flung trolleys. Park Row terminal was, by the early twentieth century, the principal gateway between Brooklyn and Manhattan, and along with the improved electric train service it fueled Brooklyn's growth as a bedroom borough to Manhattan.

Problem was, until 1908 Park Row's trolleys and els were the only direct rail links between the two boroughs, subjecting the terminal to heavy crowding. In 1908 the IRT opened its Contract Two[1] subway between Lower Manhattan and Atlantic Avenue, providing some relief, but the new subway took until 1920 to penetrate the growing residential neighborhoods east and south of downtown Brooklyn that were straining the elevated and trolley routes.

In the thirty-six years between 1908 and 1944 four events resulted in reducing the demand on the Brooklyn Bridge elevated tracks and ultimately removing those tracks completely. The first event was in 1908 with the opening of the BRT's Williamsburg Bridge subway-el tracks. The second event was in 1915 when new BRT subway routes constructed under the Dual Contracts began operating between Manhattan and Brooklyn, using the Fourth Avenue Subway, Manhattan Bridge, and Montague Street Tunnel. The Brighton, Sea Beach, and West End lines all shifted to the new routings, which included a new subway under Broadway between Lower Manhattan and 60th Street. The result was that BRT riders from these lines had direct one-fare service to any Manhattan location south of 60th Street, reducing Brooklyn Bridge elevated train traffic after 1920 to the Myrtle, Lexington, Fulton, Culver, and Fifth Avenue routes. These routes, with the exception of the Culver Line and parts of the Fulton Street and Myrtle Avenue els, were never completely rebuilt to handle steel subway cars. Thus the Lexington, Fulton, Myrtle (below Broadway) and Fifth Avenue routes were restricted to the older and lighter wooden pre–Dual Contracts car fleets. As noted in Chapter 1 the BRT became the BMT in 1923.

The third event occurred beginning in 1936, when the new IND Fulton Street subway opened between Manhattan and Brooklyn. Built directly below the old Fulton Street el, the new subway rendered the old el route redundant west of Rockaway Avenue. Much Brooklyn Bridge el traffic shifted to the new subway, which provided direct, one-fare, one-seat service to virtually all points in Manhattan right up to its northern

1. The original IRT subway from City Hall northward to Upper Manhattan and the Bronx is known as Contract One. Contract Two refers to the line from Brooklyn Bridge southward to Atlantic Avenue, following Broadway, the Joralemon Street Tunnel, Fulton Street, and Flatbush Avenue. It opened in 1905 as far as Bowling Green and in 1908 to Atlantic Avenue.

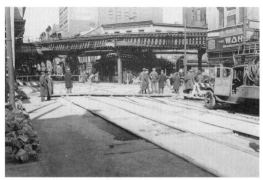

Also on March 24, 1944, new tracks are being installed at Adams and Myrtle to allow trolleys to access the Brooklyn Bridge without using the old Sands Street Station, also now closed. NYTM

December 21, 1944, looking east from City Hall Park at the site of the old Park Row terminal, now almost completely demolished except for the small area in the middle. BMT trolleys now use the former bridge el tracks and loop at a small surface terminal just beyond. To the left are the IRT Third Avenue el's City Hall terminal and below it a kiosk entrance to the Lexington Avenue subway's Brooklyn Bridge Station. On the extreme right a sign advertises Trommer's beer, a long-vanished Brooklyn-based brew. Not in the photo but still operating are the Third Avenue Railway's conduit-powered streetcars on the Third/Amsterdam route, today's M101/M103 bus, which was motorized in May 1947. NYTM

tip. Elevated passengers who reached Park Row had to transfer to IRT or BMT subway trains or bus or trolley routes to reach points north of Park Row—for a second nickel fare, as well.

The fourth event was subway unification in June 1940. When the Board of Transportation took over the BMT, it also controlled the entire Brooklyn bus and trolley system. Immediately, the board razed the old els on Fulton Street (between Brooklyn Bridge and Rockaway Avenue) and on Fifth and Third Avenues (including connections to the Culver Line), as both had parallel subway service already available. After June 1940 only two el routes remained on the Brooklyn Bridge, the Myrtle Avenue and the Lexington Avenue. Early in 1941 the Board of Transportation devised a plan to truncate the two el lines on the Brooklyn side at Jay Street and Myrtle Avenue and remove the Park

A PCC trolley on the B67/Seventh Avenue route is shown passing the old Loew's Metropolitan theater at Fulton and Smith Streets. This photo dates to 1948, when The Paradine Case, starring Gregory Peck and Ann Todd, was released. The car is headed for Park Row via the Brooklyn Bridge. NYTM

PCC #1061 is on the B69/McDonald-Vanderbilt Line about 1948, ascending the Brooklyn Bridge on a Manhattan-bound trip. NYTM

Row and Sands Street terminals and unneeded connecting trackage in Brooklyn.[2] Besides reducing redundant train routes, much-needed scrap steel could be realized. Trolleys would remain on the bridge but would shift to the old elevated tracks, requiring overhead wire to shift while the old elevated third rail was removed. Elevated passengers desiring to travel over the bridge would receive free transfers to the trolley lines at the Brooklyn end. The reverse would work for passengers leaving Manhattan.

Before this plan was effected, in 1943 the U.S. government's War Production Board almost put a stop to the elimination of the bridge el train service because the WPB was not convinced that all of the scrap steel would be donated to the government for the war effort. Finally convinced the plan was sound, the WPB allowed the end of the el service. The end came for the bridge el trains on Sunday, March 5, 1944, without ceremony or fanfare. By the end of 1944, the old Park Row terminal was gone, its steel donated to the war effort.

The trolley routes were shifted, later in 1944, to the el tracks and continued operating across the river until exactly six years and a day later. Victimized by two simultaneous events—the Board of Transportation's plan to put buses on all but three remaining Brooklyn streetcar routes in 1950 and 1951 and the city's plan to rebuild the Brooklyn Bridge for passenger cars exclusively—the last bridge streetcar, PCC car #1074 with veteran motorman James Brennan at the helm—crossed the East River just after midnight on March 6, 1950, jammed with railfans who remembered the days when Brooklyn Bridge was the only roadway link between the two boroughs.[3]

2. *New York Times* (February 15, 1941).
3. *New York Times* (March 7, 1950).

New York Times article on March 6, 1944, about the end of elevated
train service on the Brooklyn Bridge.

For many years afterward, five replacement bus routes in Brooklyn that traversed
the Brooklyn Bridge as trolleys (Flushing Avenue, Graham Avenue, Seventh Avenue,
Vanderbilt Avenue, and Smith Street) provided a free paper transfer to the IND subway
at High Street to permit a one-fare surface ride to Manhattan. This transfer privilege
ended in the 1980s.

6

1947–1948: Private to Public Bus Operations

As noted in the first chapter, the unification of the three subway systems in 1940 also put the Board of Transportation in the bus and trolley business for the first time. The BMT takeover included its far-flung surface route network, which covered all of Brooklyn, some route extensions into adjacent Queens neighborhoods, and routes over the Brooklyn, Manhattan, and Williamsburg bridges into Manhattan. Until 1947, all bus and trolley routes in New York City based outside of Brooklyn remained in the private sector. In a nineteen-month period between February 1947 and September 1948, the Board of Transportation took over private bus operators in Staten Island, Queens, and Manhattan in three separate and unrelated instances. Each time, the private operator decided quickly, and without prior warning, to cede its franchise to the board.

Staten Island was the first. Staten Island Coach Company, which held the borough's bus franchise since 1936, decided in June 1946 not to renew its franchise. A new private operator, Isle Transportation Company, whose stockholders were six prominent Staten Island businessmen, bought out Staten Island Coach and began running the island's buses on July 1, 1946. The changeover was accomplished rapidly with much last-minute paperwork; the city's Bureau of Franchises granted a temporary five-month operating permit, as did New York State's Public Service Commission, which in those days oversaw private transit bus operators statewide. Isle Transportation leased Staten Island Coach's 174 buses and agreed to continue employment for the original concern's 425 drivers, mechanics, and support personnel. Service was retained on all twenty-five routes, to the relief of the fifty thousand daily riders. The fare continued to be based on a nickel-per-zone system, unlike the other boroughs. Rides ranged in cost from five to twenty cents.

The new operation had its challenges from the very beginning. In order to maintain services, its operating permit was granted immediately but was set to expire on November 30, 1946, pending completion of application for a permanent five-year permit. Five days before the changeover, on June 25, 1946, a spectacular nine-alarm fire killed three people and destroyed the St. George Ferry Terminal, the hub of Staten Island's bus, rail, and ferry transportation. The ferry service resumed three days later using a temporary slip at St. George; bus operations were also able to resume using the existing bus ramps to access the slip, important because the majority of the bus riders were transferees to and from the ferries.

Motley collection of Isle Transportation buses (four are visible), plus a taxicab, at St. George Terminal, during the summer of 1946 when Isle operated Staten Island buses. Note that the buses are shorter than the thirty-five-foot length that would be found on heavy city routes at that time, including all other New York City boroughs. This photo was taken right after a disastrous fire destroyed the adjacent ferry terminal. Motor Bus Society

Staten Island's first postwar buses were thirty-five White Motor Company vehicles such as #600, shown above at St. George. Isle ordered these, but when delivered the Board of Transportation had already taken over, so the buses were delivered in the city's green and silver colors. Motor Bus Society

Mack #1637, a 1948 gasoline-powered thirty-five-foot bus, was part of the first group of city-purchased Staten Island vehicles; it is shown on Bay Street after leaving the ferry terminal on the Hylan Boulevard route, then R103 and today S78. Motor Bus Society

GM #4684, a TDH-5101 of 1949 vintage, was part of the second group of city-purchased buses ordered for Staten Island. It is shown at St. George in the early 1950s, on route R111/Bradley Avenue, now S57. This group totaled four hundred buses, some also assigned to Brooklyn and Queens routes. Motor Bus Society

Then on October 3, 1946, Isle Transportation's drivers and mechanics walked off the job in a contract dispute, in an effort to raise the pay for experienced personnel from $1.06 to $1.25 per hour. After eight days the strike ended and drivers went back to work after agreeing to a nine-cent increase to $1.15 hourly. The next potential crisis occurred on November 10, when Isle asked the city's Board of Estimate to impose a flat ten-cent fare in lieu of the zone system and reduce its franchise tax in order to continue operations.[1] The request was denied.

1. *New York Times* (November 11, 1946).

Ultimately Isle Transportation did not survive as a private company. On February 19, 1947, its directors notified the Board of Estimate that it could not continue operations. Isle owed $30,000 in franchise taxes to New York City and was liable for an additional $50,000 in additional labor costs in 1947 under its union agreement.[2] Thus, effective February 21, 1947, Isle's stockholders surrendered its franchise to the City of New York.

The Board of Transportation was now in the bus business for a second time. It inherited Isle's 174 well-worn prewar buses as well as an order for thirty-five yet-undelivered new White Motor Company forty-four-passenger buses, which the board paid for upon their delivery.

Staten Island's long route lengths and low population densities almost guaranteed a money-losing operation. Mass transit requires dense population patterns in order to be financially viable. Comparing Staten Island to the other boroughs will readily illustrate this concept. In 1950, Staten Island's population was 191,555 distributed on sixty square miles, or a population density of 3,193 per square mile. In the other four boroughs, 1950 population densities per square mile were 86,730 (Manhattan), 38,566 (Brooklyn), 34,554 (the Bronx), and 12,924 (Queens).

Another factor that affected the financial success of any Staten Island bus operation was the renewed availability of new private cars after World War II. Staten Island residents were much more likely to use private cars for local travel, given the suburban and semirural land use patterns in that borough.

With the takeover, the Board of Transportation created a Staten Island Bus Division, separate and distinct from its Brooklyn surface operation. The immediate reaction of the island's residents was positive, since municipal operation ended the uncertainties from a succession of private operators. In addition to the thirty-five new White buses, Staten Island received new Mack and GM buses ordered as part equipment upgrades on all Board of Transportation routes. By 1949, the old Isle buses were gone, replaced with new, larger buses that had between forty-five and fifty seats each.

In 1947 Queens streets hosted a total of nine separate bus and trolley operators. All but one was a private sector firm; the exception was a group of bus and trolley routes that were part of the Board of Transportation's Brooklyn Bus and Trolley Division. In March 1947, a month after the Staten Island system fell into the public sector, the North Shore Bus Company suddenly announced it was surrendering its franchise. The accompanying table lists Queens bus and trolley operators at that time.

North Shore was the primary surface line operator in Queens's eastern half, with a twenty-seven-route network whose primary purpose was transporting riders to and from Flushing and Jamaica. Those two communities provided subway access to Manhattan

2. *New York Times* (February 21, 1947).

Queens Bus and Trolley Operators in 1947

Operator	Routes and Locations	Year to Public Sector
NYC Board of Transportation (bus and trolley)	Western Queens extensions of Brooklyn routes, as far as Jamaica, Flushing, Maspeth, and Richmond Hill	1940—Board of Transportation Brooklyn Bus and Trolley Division
North Shore Bus	Eastern Queens subway feeders focused on Flushing and Jamaica	1947—Board of Transportation Queens Bus Division
Fifth Avenue Coach[a]	Fifth Avenue—Jackson Heights; plus Elmhurst Crosstown	1962—Manhattan and Bronx Surface Transit Operating Authority (MABSTOA)
NYC Omnibus[a]	Triboro Bridge (Manhattan–Astoria)	
Queens-Nassau Transit[b]	Central Queens north-south between Jamaica and Flushing, plus Northern Blvd. and Maspeth–LIC	2005–2006—MTA Bus Company
Steinway Omnibus[b]	Northwest Queens (Astoria and Long Island City) including Queensboro Bridge trolley	
Green Bus[c]	South Queens (Jamaica, Kew Gardens, Ozone Park, Richmond Hill, Rockaways), plus Queens Blvd.	
Triboro Coach[c]	Northwest Queens (Astoria, Woodside, Jackson Heights, Long Island City, Elmhurst, Rego Park, Forest Hills)	
Jamaica Buses[c]	South Queens (Jamaica, Far Rockaway, Ozone Park, Hollis, Queens Village)	

a. Fifth Avenue and NYC Omnibus were under common ownership; they merged in 1956.

b. Queens-Nassau and Steinway Omnibus were under common ownership since 1939. Names changed slightly over the years before the two merged as Queens Surface Corporation in 1986.

c. Green Bus owned Triboro after 1947 and Jamaica after 1949.

North Shore Bus Company Twin Coach on route Q36 in 1939, taking on a capacity load on a morning peak trip to Jamaica. The paper sign in the windshield reminds passengers that this bus runs express between 212th Street and the IND subway at 169th Street and Hillside Avenue. Motor Bus Society

In 1947, right after the Board of Transportation took over North Shore's routes, we see a lineup of three Twins, two prewar and a then-new model in the middle, on Jamaica Avenue at 169th Street near the end of the BMT elevated. The one on the left has just been repainted in the Board of Transportation's new green and silver colors. The storefronts in the background reflect Jamaica's historical role as the primary shopping area of Queens until the 1970s. Atop the first bus is a sign for the Merkel Meat Market, a chain that went out of business suddenly in 1965 after a scandal involving meat that did not meet standards for human consumption. Motor Bus Society

and were also major retail shopping hubs. North Shore's routes suffered from the same ills as the Staten Island ones—long trips, rush-hour peaking, and neighborhoods with low-density housing and vacant land, resulting in low off-peak transit usage. On March 28, 1947, in the midst of negotiations with the city to renew its franchise, North Shore Bus abruptly threw in the towel and surrendered its franchise rights to the Board of Transportation. Citing financial difficulties that prevented it from operating at a profit, North Shore's president Joseph Rauchwerger publicly blamed the nickel fare for his firm's demise. He claimed that North Shore could have continued profitably with a fare above a nickel but less than a dime.[3] The city's insistence on a five-cent fare, plus the 7 percent of

3. *New York Times* (March 29, 1947).

In 1949 the Board of Transportation purchased four hundred of these GM model 5101 buses, custom designed with a large front door to facilitate passenger loading and unloading at busy terminal points. About two hundred ran on ex–North Shore Queens routes for their entire careers; this one is brand new at the Flushing garage with its roll sign displaying BRONX; it would thus be used for route Q44 northbound trips that connected that borough with Queens. Motor Bus Society

Twenty years after North Shore Bus disappeared, the Queens Bus Division continued its major function of ferrying customers between subways and neighborhoods beyond. Taken around 1967, this photo shows afternoon rush hour riders on Roosevelt Avenue in Flushing boarding #7127, a GM 1957 model TDH5106 that served Queens Division routes for many years. It was part of the first group of NYCTA buses with fiberglass seating and push-type exit doors. This bus is on route Q13/ Flushing–Bayside–Fort Totten and is missing its right-side roll sign. NYTM

its gross receipts collected as franchise tax each year, pushed North Shore, according to Rauchwerger, into the public sector. After the Board of Transportation takeover North Shore sold its two remaining routes, which operated from Flushing to Glen Cove and Great Neck, to Schenck Transportation Company, the predominant bus operator in the northern half of Nassau County. Schenck kept the Glen Cove route until 1973, when Nassau County bought Schenck and all other privately owned bus operators operating there.

When the Board of Transportation began running North Shore's operation on March 30, 1947, it absorbed 271 buses and 840 employees. As was the case with the Staten Island operation, many buses were worn out and in need of replacement. Both eastern Queens and Staten Island, with much vacant land, stood to gain population as the postwar demand for new housing began. The low-density residential patterns pre-

Taken at 50th Street and Broadway in the late 1930s, this photo shows three separate forms of privately owned mass transit that have all become integral parts of today's city-run transit network. The bus is a Comprehensive Omnibus Mack on the M3 49th/50th Streets crosstown (M50 today), the streetcar is on Third Avenue Railway's B/Broadway route (today's M104 bus), and below the subway kiosks is the IRT Broadway–Seventh Avenue Local (today's #1 train). The Howard clothes store was a citywide chain that was known for midpriced men's clothing. Just beyond the photo is the Capitol Theatre, a first-run movie house. Motor Bus Society

dominant in those boroughs also made private autos a bigger competitor to public transit than was the case in Brooklyn, the Bronx, and Manhattan.

With the Queens and Staten Island operations joining the Board of Transportation's already large Brooklyn surface network, major bus manufacturers eagerly looked at it as a potential new customer for hundreds of new vehicles. In 1941, the Board of Transportation had leased 250 Twin Coach vehicles for its Brooklyn routes and then bought newer postwar Twin Coaches for Brooklyn in 1947–1948. But other bus manufacturers were eyeing the board as a possible customer as well.

In 1947, the Board of Transportation received its first GM diesel buses, twenty forty-five-passenger model 4506s, for use on the former North Shore routes in Queens; the private company had ordered these prior to surrendering its franchises. An additional 191 similar GM diesels were delivered to the board in 1948, all destined for Queens routes. With the postwar population expected to grow in Queens and Staten Island, the need to replace many older prewar buses, and the expectation that Brooklyn's remaining streetcars would ultimately become bus routes, General Motors was convinced that the Board of Transportation could become a large customer and was to be treated with care. The board requested two unique bus models, nine hundred units in all. GM agreed to engineer and build them, and the models were never built for any other operator. The first group, five hundred model 4510 thirty-five-foot buses, 102 inches wide, were assigned to Brooklyn routes exclusively. While they contained the normal forty-four seats in a thirty-five-foot bus, their extra six inches beyond the standard bus width was designed to provide more standing room on crowded, short-haul routes. These buses were the first large order of 102-inch-wide buses for New York City. For many years, such vehicles could not operate on interstate highways anywhere in the United States, a restriction that was completely eliminated in the 1970s.

The second group, four hundred model 5101 buses, forty feet long and ninety-six inches wide, were specifically designed for Staten Island and Queens routes that fed ferry and subway terminals. They were equipped with double-width front doors to speed loading and unloading large groups of people at one location. These buses were delivered between the fall of 1948 and the spring of 1949. About one hundred ran in Staten Island when new, and about two hundred were assigned to the Queens Division. The remaining one hundred units were assigned to Brooklyn routes, and they re-equipped streetcar routes there in the first six months of 1949.

Manhattan, long the bastion of the city's best-known private bus operator, Fifth Avenue Coach Company, found itself with a minor bus crisis in the early fall of 1948. This time it was two small companies under the common ownership of Samuel Rosoff, Comprehensive Omnibus and East Side Omnibus. Rosoff, called "Subway Sam" because he made a fortune as a tunnel contractor for the original IND subway, was politically well connected and a self-made millionaire.[4] Comprehensive owned three crosstown routes (Madison-Chambers Streets, 49th-50th Streets, and 65th-66th Streets); East Side owned three north-south lines (York, First, and Second Avenues). While the city takeover in this case was almost unnoticed in the media, it too was fraught with maneuverings and drama. The Comprehensive/East Side management, like its counterparts on the city's other private bus and trolley companies, had long maintained that profitable operation was not possible under the nickel fare. During most of 1948, Rosoff was lobbying the Board of Estimate for a two-cent raise to seven cents while at the same time quietly negotiating to turn over the franchises to the Board of Transportation. Finally on September 22, 1948, the city granted an interim one-cent raise to six cents a ride. Claiming the one-cent increase was inadequate, Comprehensive/East Side immediately surrendered its franchise, and the Board of Transportation began operating its new Manhattan Bus Division on September 24, using the existing Comprehensive/East Side garage on East 100th Street. The city paid $700,000 for 197 buses and the garage.[5] Ironically, when the Comprehensive/East Side customers began riding on city-operated buses, they paid the seven-cent fare that the city had denied the private operator.

4. Rosoff died in 1951 at age sixty-eight. He was a self-made, self-taught millionaire who came to the United States from Russia at age twelve. The *New York Times*, in its April 10, 1951, obituary, quoted him as saying "I haven't got any education." The article noted that he built canals, tunnels, and roads in many countries.

5. *New York Times* (September 24, 1948).

Just before it ceded its franchise to the Board of Transportation, Comprehensive/East Side bought this Mack demonstrator bus, shown on the M13 First Avenue route at 125th Street, in 1948. Despite the lettering on the side this route was part of East Side Omnibus; both were commonly owned. Motor Bus Society

In 1948 the Board of Transportation obtained 115 Mack C45 diesel buses including #5068. Originally part of a Surface Transportation Corporation order for its Yonkers lines, the board bought them because of Surface's ongoing financial problems. Although this one is shown signed for a Brooklyn route, virtually all buses in this series ran on the former Comprehensive/East Side routes from 1948 until 1957, which had become the Board of Transportation (and later NYCTA) Manhattan Bus Division. Motor Bus Society

In 1950, the Board of Transportation purchased four hundred Mack C50 diesels, which it custom designed; some were assigned to Manhattan Division routes. #5235 is shown at Madison and Rutgers Streets on the Lower East Side in 1951, with a very typical street scene surrounding it. The Manhattan Bridge looms in the background, and at right is the Madison Street entrance to the IND subway's East Broadway Station, today served by the F train. Motor Bus Society

While these six routes were still dwarfed by Manhattan's biggest bus operator, the combined Fifth Avenue Coach–New York City Omnibus operation, the Board of Transportation's absorption of Comprehensive/East Side was the first time that city-operated buses operated on Manhattan routes. In June 1951 First and Second Avenues became paired, one-way thoroughfares, and Route M15, which has served this combined route since then, has become the busiest urban bus route in North America.

As was the case with the acquired Staten Island and Queens properties, the Board of Transportation wasted little time in reequipping the Manhattan Division with new equipment. In early 1949 a group of 115 Mack forty-five-passenger diesel buses, originally destined for the Yonkers routes of the Surface Transportation Corporation, became board property when Surface could not finance their purchase. Most were assigned to Manhattan routes. In 1950–1951 four hundred additional, new fifty-passenger

Mack buses, built to a custom design, were delivered and placed in service on Board of Transportation routes in Manhattan and Brooklyn; later they served Staten Island routes as well.[6]

Its acquisition of the Staten Island, Queens, and Manhattan routes, joined to its already existing Brooklyn operation, made the Board of Transportation the city's biggest single bus operator, dwarfing the remaining private companies in Manhattan, the Bronx, and Queens. The city's bus situation would stay stable for the next fourteen years; it would not be until 1962 that the public sector operation added another large chunk of bus routes. This event, Fifth Avenue Coach Lines' sudden disappearance in 1962 after new management took control, is the subject of Chapter 16.

6. This group of Mack buses were known as "Bingham Macks" because the vehicles incorporated custom design features that were the brainchild of Colonel Sidney H. Bingham, then the chairman of the Board of Transportation. Chapter 8 has more about the "Bingham Macks."

7

1948: Goodbye to the Nickel

It was the bane of their existence for many New York politicians, a sacred cow to the riding public, and an ambivalent issue with the labor unions that represented the subway and bus workers. "It" is the nickel transit fare, which lasted on the New York City subways for forty-four years, from October 27, 1904, when the first subway opened, until July 1, 1948, when the fare finally doubled to a dime. If one were to include the Manhattan elevated lines, which charged a nickel as early as 1886, that plebian tariff lasted for an amazing sixty-two years.[1]

In 1913 New York City and the two private rapid transit operating companies, the IRT and BRT, signed the famous Dual Contracts agreements. Under these agreements a five-cent fare was mandated, which ironically the two companies were pleased with, because each felt that such a provision would end any pressure to *lower* the fare. A few years later came World War I and the resulting postwar inflation, which drove up the companies' operating costs. The riding public, however, considered the "nickel ride" an entitlement that they would simply not give up. Mayor John Hylan, who took office in 1918, made the nickel fare a linchpin of his administration and a cudgel he used against the IRT and BRT. The city's insistence on retaining the nickel fare became a political hot potato that affected every mayor from Hylan to William O'Dwyer, who took office in 1946. During O'Dwyer's first term, the historic nickel barrier was finally breached, but not before years of contentious, vociferous, and often bitter debates about the merits and problems of charging five cents for a ride that could be twenty miles long from Wakefield in the Bronx to East New York in Brooklyn.

The basic problem of the nickel fare was that it did not cover all operating costs, except between 1942 and 1946 when heavy wartime riding generated an operating surplus. The city's budget was required to make up the difference between fare revenue and total operating costs by using tax revenues. This was the case during the first eight years of the Independent Subway, beginning in 1932, and then was exacerbated in 1940 when the city bought out the BMT and IRT under the subway unification program. The IND even considered raising its fare prior to unification because of the operating deficits.

1. Robert Reed, *The New York Elevated* (Cranbury, NJ: A. S. Barnes, 1978), 128.

The Dual Contracts Explained

The Dual Contracts of 1913 were probably the most important event in the history of the entire subway system. In 1898 the present five-borough system was established, joining Brooklyn, Queens, and Staten Island to the then-existing City of New York (Manhattan and the Bronx). In 1910, Manhattan's population peaked at 2,331,542, or 49 percent of the overall five-borough total of 4,766,883; by comparison its twenty-two square miles represented only 7.2 percent of the five boroughs' 315 square miles. The first subway had opened between 1904 and 1908, primarily serving Manhattan with extensions into the Bronx and Brooklyn. It was clear that new subway construction had to be coordinated with decongesting desperately overcrowded Manhattan, as the other four boroughs had thousands of acres that could absorb new residential development. An orderly expansion of the nascent subway system was required.

According to the transportation historian Peter Derrick's book *Tunneling to the Future*, in 1911 Manhattan Borough President George McAneny stepped into this leadership vacuum about making decisions about new subway routes. McAneny proposed that the city government designate and construct new subways. This idea became the basis for the Dual Contracts, so-called because two private companies, the IRT and BRT, agreed to lease and operate specific groups of new routes, primarily based on borough geography. The IRT was the sole operator in Manhattan north of 60th Street and in the Bronx. The BMT received the lion's share of Brooklyn and Queens routes, including shared service with the IRT on lines to Astoria and Corona under a unique joint operating agreement. In Manhattan between 60th Street and South Ferry, each company received a parallel route, despite the IRT's initial contention that it had exclusive rights to this territory.

After long and sometimes acrimonious negotiations, the two companies signed the Dual Contracts agreements in March 1913. The financial arrangements underlying the contracts stipulated that a five-cent fare be charged. While the merits of this fare ceiling have been debated ever since, the fact is that the Dual Contracts doubled the city's rapid-transit mileage, tripled its passenger capacity, and allowed families by the hundreds of thousands to leave Manhattan's overcrowded tenements and live in newer housing in the Bronx, Brooklyn, and Queens. Regardless of where these people lived, they still had to pay only five cents to reach Manhattan by subway or elevated, an issue that was a sacred cow in New York politics until 1948.

An example of how the nickel fare was a hot-button issue in the late thirties and early forties can be gleaned from the classic guidebook *WPA Guide to New York City*, published in 1939. A chapter about the subway and elevated lines concludes with the sentences: "The five cent fare—a recurring issue in municipal politics—is not likely to be increased in the immediate or distant future. The New Yorker is extremely sensitive on this point."[2]

2. Federal Writers Project, *WPA Guide to New York City* (New York: Federal Writers Project, 1939), 406.

This sensitivity made an impression, naturally, on politicians. One staunch advocate of the nickel fare was Stanley M. Isaacs (1882–1962), a liberal Republican who was Manhattan borough president from 1938 through 1941 and then a city council member until his death. Isaacs argued that the nickel fare gave poor families mobility throughout the city and allowed everyone to enjoy its benefits and cultural activities.[3] Quoted in *722 Miles* by Clifton Hood, Isaacs called the subway the "highway of the masses." Isaacs was not the stereotypical political clubhouse type—he was an unabashedly honest man who truly believed what he said and practiced what he preached.

The other side of the coin (pun intended) was the Committee of Fifteen, led by the prominent Republican attorney Paul Windels (1885–1967). He served as New York City's corporation counsel in Mayor LaGuardia's first term (1934–1937) and then returned to private law practice. During World War II, when subway crowding and physical conditions reached a low point, Windels argued that a ten-cent fare made sense because it would yield enough revenues to provide better service than was possible with a nickel tariff, particularly by replacing the old, worn out trains of early twentieth-century vintage with modern new ones.[4] In 1944, Windels made a radio address in which he all but pleaded with his former boss to raise the fare, arguing that "lousy service" with the nickel fare could be replaced with good service under a dime fare.

An objective view of the entire situation was an article in the *New York Times Magazine* on Sunday, March 10, 1946. Murray Schumach's "What's Wrong with the Subway? What Isn't?" was a critical look at the underground labyrinth that New Yorkers rode twice daily. The biggest complaints were dirty stations, dirty car windows, and incomprehensible maps in the cars. Often the maps only showed one of the three subway divisions. Another person noted that the "sometimes it's hard to believe that the same city owns the Independent and the IRT." That last comment was a reflection of the relative newness of the IND lines (then between six and fourteen years old) versus the forty-plus-year-old IRT and even older elevated lines it controlled. The most telling point was that every subway rider interviewed for the article was in favor of a fare increase as long as the system was made more comfortable and attractive, meaning newer cars and better stations. One person suggested an eight-cent fare; another idea was two rides for fifteen cents.

Whatever the case, the nickel fare was definitely living its last years. While Mayor LaGuardia's "we got a good deal" proclamation was an argument for retaining the nickel, much of the operating surplus that was earned through 1945 was generated by heavy World War II ridership and the rationing of gasoline and tires. These conditions were artificial and would end when World War II ended. The change came quickly: inflationary pressures made postwar operating expenses rise faster than fare revenue,

3. Clifton Hood, *722 Miles* (Baltimore, Md.: Johns Hopkins University Press, 1993), 245.
4. Ibid., 250.

resulting in the wartime surplus becoming a deficit after 1946 that would have to be closed by using the city's operating budget. When the fare finally went up, New York was the last major city still charging a nickel transit fare.[5] Other major cities charged higher fares, in some cases for many years.

In Boston, the Commonwealth of Massachusetts had taken control of the Boston Elevated Railway Company in 1919 to forestall that company's bankruptcy. Part of the arrangement was a ten-cent fare on the system's subways and els. In September 1947 a new public agency, the Metropolitan Transit Authority (MTA), took over the "Boston El" and continued the dime fare. Chicago was a similar story, in which a new public agency, the Chicago Transit Authority (CTA), took over two large private firms— Chicago Rapid Transit and Chicago Surface Lines—in October 1947 and raised the fare from ten to twelve cents. San Francisco's Municipal Railway (Muni), a city-owned system, took over a competing, larger private firm, the Market Street Railway, in September 1944 and immediately began charging a flat seven-cent fare on the entire system. By 1948 Muni was charging a dime as well.

In the twenty-first century a cost increase from five to ten cents may seem inconsequential, but it still represented a 100 percent jump. The early months of 1948 saw much posturing between the New York City and New York State governments over the subway fare issue. Since the Board of Transportation was an agency directly reportable to Mayor O'Dwyer, its budget was part of the overall city budget and was therefore sensitive to tax revenues and state aid. For a while in early 1948 it appeared that New York would adopt an eight-cent fare, and there even was a proposal for the U.S. government to mint a new eight-cent coin that would be useful to many urban transit systems besides New York's. At that time New York's private bus and trolley operators were posturing to raise their fares from five to eight cents, which would require New York State Public Service Commission approval.

One small, related aside, reported in the *New York Times* on June 3, 1948, was that the Board of Transportation had sold ten million tokens that the old IRT had minted in 1928 in anticipation of a fare raise that never occurred. The city realized over $21,000 from the sale of these tokens, which were melted down after the sale to keep them out of circulation.[6]

The eight-cent coin proposal did not last long, but pressure to raise the fare continued. Finally, Mayor O'Dwyer announced on April 20, 1948, that fares on the city-owned subways, elevateds, and surface lines would be raised on July 1, 1948, to ten cents on subways and elevateds and seven cents on Board of Transportation bus and trolley routes. A twelve-cent combination fare for rides involving both rail and surface modes was also established. Details are shown opposite:

5. *New York Times* (June 30, 1948).
6. *New York Times* (June 3, 1948).

New York Times (April 20, 1948) article headline, announcing a fare increase on July 1.

- Ten cents on subway and elevated lines, payable by inserting a dime into existing turnstiles.
- Seven cents on the Board of Transportation's bus and trolley routes in Brooklyn, Staten Island, Queens, and Manhattan. Privately owned bus and trolley lines in the Bronx (Third Avenue Transit/Surface Transportation), Queens (Steinway Omnibus, Queens Transit, Triboro Coach, Green Bus, and Jamaica Bus) and Manhattan (New York City Omnibus, Surface Transportation, Avenue B and East Broadway) would continue to charge five cents until their fares could be increased, which required action by the New York State Public Service Commission. This did not occur until later in 1948. Manhattan's Fifth Avenue Coach Company already charged ten cents, as it had for many years.
- Twelve-cent combination fare for trips requiring both subways/elevateds and bus/trolley lines in the Bronx, Brooklyn, Queens, and Staten Island, at designated transfer points. The Bronx transfer locations included 207th Street in Upper Manhattan, where the A train connected with two Surface Transportation Bronx routes. Staten Island's bus transfer point was actually at South Ferry or Whitehall Street in Manhattan, where passengers transferred between bus and subway via the ferry crossing.

The thought was that since many bus/trolley trips were of short duration, those passengers who transferred to subways should be charged a smaller increase than the longer subway and elevated trips. The twelve-cent combination fare was a means of helping two-mode users, preventing a new fare of fifteen or seventeen cents for such trips. A passenger boarding a surface vehicle desiring to transfer to rapid transit would pay twelve cents and be issued a paper transfer good at a specific subway/elevated transfer point. Passengers exiting the subway at a transfer point would purchase a two-cent transfer inside the station turnstile area that would be good only on designated connecting bus or trolley lines at that location. The twelve-cent combo fare was short lived but represented the only time prior to the 1997 Metrocard free transfers that trips requiring subways and surface vehicles required fewer than two full fares. The images in this chapter illustrate examples of transfers that passengers would buy inside subway or el stations that permitted a continuing trip on a bus or trolley for a total twelve-cent tariff.

Board of Transportation notice of fare increases effective July 1, 1948. The nickel transit fare, a New York institution that dated back to nineteenth-century elevated lines, was finally history. Author's photograph, 2010

IND division 1948 map, showing transfer privileges available for the twelve-cent combination fare. Author's photograph, 2010

Examples of subway-to-surface line transfers available under the twelve-cent combination fare implemented in 1948. The image on the left is for the IRT Flushing Line. The image on the right is for the IND stations on the A and D trains in Upper Manhattan and the Bronx. Prior to exiting the paid area of the subway, transferring passengers bought these tickets from vending machines for two cents apiece. Once on the street, the appropriate connecting bus or trolley route would accept these in lieu of a cash fare. www.thejoekorner.com.

The first day of the changeover was a Thursday, but the effect was somewhat mitigated because the next day was the beginning of the July 4 weekend. There were some snarls: turnstiles jammed, and many riders did not understand the details of the new intermodal transfers.[7]

New York Times (July 2, 1948) article describing the first day of the ten-cent subway fare and twelve-cent combination fare.

A positive result of the 1948 fare increase was the establishment of fourteen locations where free transfers were created between two or three subway divisions, at locations where prior to July 1 transferring passengers had to pay a second nickel. These locations included 168th Street–Broadway (IRT and IND), 59th Street–Columbus Circle (IRT and IND), 59th Street–Lexington Avenue (IRT and BMT), Times Square (IRT and BMT), 34th Street–Broadway (IND and BMT), 14th Street–Union Square (IRT and BMT), 14th Street–8th Avenue (IND and BMT), Park Place–Chambers Street (IRT and IND), Chambers Street–Brooklyn Bridge (IRT and BMT), Fulton Street–Broadway Nassau (IRT, IND, and BMT), Court Street–Borough Hall (IRT and BMT), Broadway Junction–Eastern Parkway (IND and BMT), Metropolitan Avenue–Lorimer Street (IND and

7. *New York Times* (July 2, 1948).

BMT), and 74th Street–Roosevelt Avenue/Jackson Heights (IRT and IND). At those locations transferring passengers now had the benefit of a free interchange and no effective fare increase.

The 1948 fare increases were the only time that New York had separate fare levels for rapid transit and surface lines. On July 1, 1950, the Board of Transportation raised its bus and trolley fare from seven to ten cents, matching the subways. The twelve-cent combination fare was increased to fifteen cents the same day. Those combination fares were eliminated on July 1, 1952, subsequently requiring a double fare (twenty cents) for trips involving rapid transit and surface routes. As financial pressures continued, the fare was raised to fifteen cents, requiring the use of a new token, in July 1953 (see Chapter 10). By this time the Board of Transportation was gone, and a new independent public agency, the New York City Transit Authority, was placed in charge of the subways and the city-owned bus and trolley lines.

8

1947–1956: Final Decade for Brooklyn Trolleys

When 1947 dawned, Brooklyn's surface riders were still likely to be boarding trolleys on a daily basis, which encompassed thirty-six of the sixty-two major surface routes that crisscrossed the Borough of Churches. Trolleys claimed the traditional heavy routes such as Flatbush Avenue, Nostrand Avenue, and Smith Street–Coney Island Avenue. Annual ridership on the borough's entire surface network—bus and trolley—peaked at 534 million fares collected, an imposing figure. Trolley routes totaled about two hundred miles; bus routes covered another 113 miles.

Now that World War II was over and civilian vehicle production had resumed, the Board of Transportation was faced with some important decisions regarding the re-equipping of Brooklyn's surface rolling stock. Because Mayor LaGuardia had forced the BMT to abandon plans to purchase additional PCC trolleys before 1940 (see Chapter 1), the system was facing the prospect of replacing over a thousand trolley cars purchased between 1923 and 1931 that would all reach between twenty and thirty years of service in the early 1950s. Twenty years of service was considered the normal service life for an urban streetcar, without a major rebuilding. It was common practice for the private companies to depreciate the cars over twenty years. The only cars under a dozen years old were the hundred PCC cars of 1936. The two solutions were either buy new trolleys or substitute new buses, but any decision would require large-scale purchases and a long-term commitment to that vehicle type. One idea in the mix was to convert some moderately heavy trolley car lines to trolley coaches in order to take advantage of preexisting electrical substations and overhead wire systems, with the understanding that trolley coach routes required work to construct an additional wire for the return current flow. Until 1948, the only trolley coach route in Brooklyn was on Cortelyou Road, a short route with an eight-vehicle fleet purchased in the early 1930s.

It is important to understand that in the immediate postwar years the issue of trolleys versus buses for heavy-duty urban routes was hotly debated in many cities. New York was hardly alone. Philadelphia, Pittsburgh, Baltimore, Washington, St. Louis, and Toronto retained conventional street-running trolleys for the majority of their heavy routes for many years afterward. New York, Buffalo, Detroit, Chicago, and Montreal all saw trolleys vanish by 1959.

William O'Dwyer became mayor in 1946, succeeding Fiorello LaGuardia. Heavy wartime usage had left the subway system in very poor physical condition, both its rolling stock and basic infrastructure. Bigger transit issues than the future of Brooklyn trolleys occupied the mayor, even though he was a Brooklyn resident. As was described in Chapter 7, the historic "nickel ride" barrier was broken as the subway fare went to a dime during O'Dwyer's first term. At the beginning of O'Dwyer's tenure, Brooklyn's surface system comprised 1,141 trolleys and 546 diesel, gasoline, and trolley buses.

The managers at the Board of Transportation continued the pro-bus policies inherited from Mayor LaGuardia. From late 1947 until mid-1949, twelve Brooklyn trolley routes were converted to rubber-tired vehicles. Included were six in the northern part of the borough that took advantage of the existing overhead wires and substations and became trolley coaches during 1948, after a brief period as temporary motor buses to enable construction of double-wire overhead. Two hundred new trolley coaches from St. Louis Car Company were purchased to equip these routes and to reequip the original Cortelyou Road line with the new coaches. The new trolley coach routes were St. Johns Place, Bergen Street, Graham Avenue, Flushing Avenue, Tompkins Avenue, and Lorimer Street. Originally it was planned to expand trolley coaches to additional routes, so the new fleet had roll sign curtains that reflected routes that would never see those vehicles.

The original bus fleet was completely renewed as well, as the motley collection of over five hundred pre–World War II gasoline and diesel vehicles were all scrapped by the end of 1948. Included were the 250 Twin Coach buses leased in 1941, 190 of which had been converted from gasoline to diesel power. None fared well under the heavy traffic of World War II and were not retained. In 1946–1947, four groups of new gasoline-powered postwar Twin Coaches, totaling about 350 buses, were installed on Brooklyn routes. These included fifty buses inherited from North Shore Bus Company in Queens that were transferred to Brooklyn after the Board of Transportation took over North Shore in March 1947.

The Twins were only the beginning. The Board of Transportation purchased 115 gasoline-powered forty-four-passenger buses from Mack Truck in 1947–1948 that initially operated in Brooklyn before spending the majority of their careers on Staten Island routes, where the Board of Transportation had inherited the bus system in February 1947 (see Chapter 6). The most significant additions to Brooklyn's postwar bus fleet before 1950 were six hundred new General Motors diesel buses that appeared in 1948–1949, encompassing two large orders of two unique vehicles. Five hundred model 4510s, thirty-five-foot buses 102 inches wide, arrived in 1948 and were all assigned to Brooklyn Division routes; they replaced both trolleys and all remaining prewar buses. Following the 4510s, four hundred equally unique model 5101 buses came in late 1948 and 1949. These buses, forty feet long but ninety-six inches wide, were primarily destined for Queens and Staten Island routes that delivered large numbers of com-

Flushing–Ridgewood trolley meets a Twin Coach bus that is covering the last mile of the route, about 1948, given the street and sewer construction along Lawrence Street in Flushing (now College Point Boulevard). NYTM

A BMT trolley is on the Junction Boulevard Line, close to its last day of service (August 25, 1949). Photo is on the 94th Street Bridge over Grand Central Parkway at LaGuardia Airport. A Triboro Coach bus on the left is on route Q33, now part of MTA Bus Company. NYTM

A new Mack bus passes one of the last Jamaica Avenue trolleys on November 30, 1947, the day buses took over. BMT elevated is overhead. NYTM

Mayor O'Dwyer (with overcoat open) and other officials inspecting brand-new GMC model 5101 buses in 1949. These buses served routes in Brooklyn, Queens, and Staten Island when new. Later in their careers they served Manhattan routes, both NYCTA and after 1962 on MABSTOA routes. NYTM

Two GMC 4510s are on Prospect Park West at 15th Street, Brooklyn, in 1958, the year Tempest was released. The Sanders Theatre survives today, renamed the Pavilion, although it has recently closed. NYTM

A parade of GMC 4510s on Court Street in downtown Brooklyn, early 1950s. Unused trolley tracks are still in the pavement. Borough Hall is in the background. NYTM

Mack bus #5359 on the B41/Flatbush Avenue route outside Flatbush Depot about 1952. Known as "Bingham" Macks after the Board of Transportation chairman, many of these buses replaced trolleys on ten heavy Brooklyn routes in 1950–1951. They were a customized design. NYTM

Interior shot of a custom-designed "Bingham" Mack, showing the S-shaped seating and hooks along the sidewall designed to carry stretchers in the event the bus was needed as a wartime ambulance. NYTM

muters to subway and ferry terminals, which accounted for their extra large front doors and resulting short wheelbases. About one hundred 5101s were assigned when new to Brooklyn routes beginning in early 1949 and were found on newly converted trolley routes, such as DeKalb, Gates, and Vanderbilt Avenues. Brooklyn's new GM bus fleet was deemed successful and convinced the Board of Transportation's managers that additional trolley coach conversions would not be needed. Diesel buses would be the vehicle of choice.

While it appeared that the die was cast in the ultimate future of Brooklyn's surface routes, there were still fifteen trolley routes running, generally some of the system's heaviest haulers, such as Flatbush, Nostrand, and Church Avenues. As 1950 dawned, it was announced that these lines would be retained as trolleys for an indefinite period. Some even received new wire and track to ensure continued safe operation. In March 1950 trolley service ended on five routes that crossed the Brooklyn Bridge, but the cars continued to run in Brooklyn itself. Passengers who formerly rode trolleys into Manhattan were given free transfers to IND subway trains at High Street–Brooklyn Bridge Station; return transfers were sold only at the Broadway-Nassau Station outside of the paid area. This policy ensured that any passenger making a round trip using a transfer had to begin any Brooklyn-bound trip at Broadway-Nassau (today's Fulton Street Station).

Later in 1950 decisions were made that ensured that Brooklyn's surface line routes would ultimately be 100 percent rubber tire. The Board of Transportation's new chairman, Sidney Bingham (1894–1980), was as pro-bus as Mayor LaGuardia and decided to accelerate the streetcar replacements. In 1950 he arranged with Mack Truck to design and fabricate four hundred customized forty-foot, fifty-passenger diesel buses, many of which replaced the trolleys on all but three remaining Brooklyn routes. The "Bingham

1947 Twin #1568 poses on a Brooklyn street when new. These buses, all gasoline powered, dominated service on many southern Brooklyn routes from 1947 until 1956. Their demise came when NYCTA determined that diesel power was superior for urban buses. NYTM

St. Louis Car Company trolley coach #3074, early 1950s on the B45/St. Johns Place route passing the Long Island Rail Road terminal at Atlantic and Flatbush Avenues. Two hundred of these vehicles served Brooklyn routes from 1948 until 1960. A Bickford's cafeteria, long a New York staple for basic food, dominated the street level of the terminal. Corned beef hash was thirty cents, as noted in the window ad. NYTM

Macks," as they became known, incorporated design features that would make them convertible to ambulances in case of a foreign attack. This was the early 1950s, and Cold War hysteria was at its height. Civil defense was a big topic in those days, much like antiterrorism is today. Extra-wide doors were provided to allow stretchers to be placed inside the bus, which could be hung from hooks placed along the inside walls. A unique S-shaped transverse seat was installed, ostensibly to allow window-seat passengers easier egress. The ambulance features were never used except in mock drills when the buses were new. The S-shaped seats were not satisfactory and never replicated in subsequent bus orders from any other bus operator; some buses had conventional straight-back seats installed as replacements.

Design flaws notwithstanding, between August 1950 and May 1951 ten heavy Brooklyn trolley lines, including Flatbush, Nostrand, and Utica Avenues, were changed to bus operation using a good portion of the four hundred "Bingham Macks." Now the trolley network was whittled down to three lines—Church, McDonald, and Coney Island Avenues—where the hundred PCC cars could provide all of the service out of the Ninth Avenue Depot. An additional twenty 1920s vintage 8000 series double-ended ex-BMT trolleys were also retained to provide a short-turn service that required use of a switch in the middle of McDonald Avenue to enable cars to change direction. This service ran until 1954, before the IND subway's D train was extended along McDonald Avenue on the Culver Elevated route. PCC cars were single-ended and required turning loops at the ends of the routes, making them unusable for this route variation.

GMC bus #4358 at the northwestern corner of East 16th Street and Avenue U in February 1949, with the BMT Brighton Line station to the left. Cooky's was a well-known chain of Brooklyn restaurants in the 1950s and 1960s that had a number of outlets adjacent to Brighton Line stations. NYTM

Trolley #8209, a 1920s vintage Peter Witt car, on the Nostrand Avenue route at Eastern Parkway, marooned after the December 1947 blizzard. NYTM

Trolley #8276 on the Fifth Avenue route, another 1920s vintage Peter Witt, on Atlantic Avenue heading westbound to the waterfront as it crosses Flatbush Avenue in 1948. NYTM

The PCC cars would reach their twenty-year anniversary in October 1956. After that they would reach the age at which conventional wisdom dictated replacement or rebuilding. Citing statistics that diesel buses cost 88 cents per mile to operate, compared to $1.34 for trolleys, steps were taken to retire the PCCs and convert their routes to bus as well. In November 1955 the long Coney Island Avenue route was changed over, without requiring new buses. Enough of the 1948 vintage model 4510 GM buses were available, used because ridership had been falling since the fifteen-cent fare was introduced in 1953.

PCC trolleys remained for their final eleven months on the Church and McDonald Avenues. The death knell for both occurred, with a touch of eerie irony, in the early morning hours of Halloween, Wednesday, October 31, 1956. A combination of GM 4510s and newly delivered Mack C49 diesel buses took over Church Avenue. McDonald

PCC trolley #1004 on the B35 Church Avenue route in the early 1950s, shown entering Bristol Street Loop in East New York, the east end of this route. NYTM

An 8000 series Peter Witt car on the Flushing–Ridgewood Line meets a PCC on a fan trip in 1949, shortly before the route was motorized, on 41st Avenue in Flushing. NYTM

#6141 is on the Flatbush Avenue Line shortly before its 1951 motorization, about to begin the long trek from downtown Brooklyn to Avenue U or East 71st Street. NYTM

Avenue trolleys were retired without any replacement bus service below Ditmas Avenue, because two years earlier the Culver Line elevated directly above had been rehabilitated with longer platforms and connected to the IND subway at Church Avenue, providing faster service along the same route.

However, 1956 was not the complete end of electric-powered surface lines in Brooklyn. The seven trolley coach routes were reduced to six when the isolated Cortelyou Road line was changed to diesel bus the same day the trolleys vanished on Church and McDonald Avenues. St. Johns Place became a bus in March 1959, and the remaining five routes were converted on July 27, 1960, upon the delivery of NYCTA's second group of GMC New Look 5301 buses to Brooklyn. These buses, which became ubiquitous all over New York in the 1960s, are described in detail in Chapter 10.

Thus in the twenty years after Brooklyn's surface routes became part of the Board of Transportation, the system morphed from predominantly electric rail to entirely diesel bus. New York's very last streetcar, the unique Queensboro Bridge shuttle between Manhattan, Welfare (now Roosevelt) Island, and Long Island City, hung on until April 1957, when it too succumbed to buses. Unlike the Brooklyn routes, this route was part of the Steinway Transit Corporation, a private concern. Steinway's successor firm, Queens Surface Corporation, was part of the group of four Queens bus operators that remained in private hands until the MTA took over their operations in 2005–2006.

9

1950: Farewell, Lexington Avenue

Lexington Avenue in Manhattan is New York's most heavily used subway trunk route, but it is not the only street of that name within the five boroughs. Because Brooklyn was its own city before 1898, many of its street names are the same as those in Manhattan. Broadway, Third Avenue, Fifth Avenue, Park Avenue, and Fulton Street are some well-known examples. Another is Lexington Avenue, which today is a minor residential thoroughfare in the Fort Greene and Bedford-Stuyvesant neighborhoods. Beginning in 1885, it was the route of the very first elevated train line in the then City of Brooklyn, the progenitor of a large route network, totaling over sixty route miles, that covered the northern and southwestern sections of Kings County by the early twentieth century. Originally steam powered, the Lexington line along with its sister routes in Brooklyn converted to electric power in 1900.

Lexington Avenue el trains were among the first to provide through service across the Brooklyn Bridge beginning in 1898, providing a one-seat ride between the two biggest boroughs of the new Greater New York. By the late nineteenth century Lexington Avenue was united with Brooklyn's entire elevated and surface rail network under the Brooklyn Rapid Transit Company umbrella, which became the BMT in 1923. In 1940 the BMT became part of the newly unified Board of Transportation system, which immediately began removing some of Brooklyn's older el lines. The Lexington and sister parallel line along Myrtle Avenue survived this initial purge and were thus the last remaining elevated lines to cross the Brooklyn Bridge when that service was ended in March 1944. Afterward, Lexington and Myrtle trains both terminated at Bridge/Jay Street in downtown Brooklyn, where free transfers were available to streetcar routes that still plied the Brooklyn Bridge, enabling el riders to reach Park Row.

Ridership declined on the Lexington Avenue line after its Manhattan link was severed, and the decline continued after World War II. In April 1950 the Board of Transportation announced that the line would close. Daily ridership had dwindled to about 7,300, compared to 13,000 in 1948. Change booth clerks were not assigned to the line's eight stations between 9 PM and 5 AM because of the low patronage, so customers paid their fares directly to the train conductors. Parallel elevated service was retained on Myrtle Avenue, and the Board of Transportation cited bus routes on Gates and DeKalb Avenues as other travel alternatives for the Lexington line's customers.

Lexington el train turning from Myrtle to Grand Avenue on its way to 111th Street, about 1950. NYTM

DeKalb Avenue Station a few days before the el closed. The sign to the left of the ads announces the imminent end of service. The ads to the right are a potpourri of transit advertising in 1950: a hospital fund, soft drinks, beer, and brassieres. NYTM

Lexington el train on a fan trip in 1949. As rumors of the line's closing intensified, train buffs arranged trips before it would become too late. NYTM

Train near the Pratt Institute campus about 1950, above Grand Avenue as it transitions between Myrtle and Lexington. One of the thousands of New York City candy stores of the era is visible just below the el on the right. NYTM

Turning from Grand onto Lexington Avenue, 1950. NYTM

Nostrand Avenue Station about 1950 with a northbound trolley about to dive under the el, heading toward the Williamsburg Bridge. Brownstones and a Mercury convertible complete the period photo. NYTM

In 1950 a train bound for 111th Street and Jamaica Avenue is atop Grand Avenue. A block ahead it will go through the Pratt Institute campus; the large smokestack belongs to the campus power plant. NYTM

El train heading toward Bridge Jay Street, turning from Broadway onto Lexington Ave. NYTM

One long-forgotten footnote of the Lexington Avenue Elevated is that right up to the end it was actually three services. After the Brooklyn Bridge link was closed in 1944, base service (called Lexington Avenue) operated between Bridge/Jay and Eastern Parkway, using the Myrtle, Lexington, and Broadway el routes. In rush hours the Lexington trains operated eastward as far as 111th Street and Jamaica Avenue, where a middle track was used to turn the trains. A third service called Fulton-Lexington operated between Bridge-Jay and Grant Avenue in East New York on the Fulton Street el, thus giving Fulton riders service to Lexington Avenue stations as well. East of Eastern Parkway, Fulton-Lexington trains operated along Pitkin Avenue to Grant Avenue at the Brooklyn-Queens line.

The last Lexington Avenue el train operated on Friday night, October 13, 1950, leaving Bridge/Jay at 9:25 PM and arriving at Eastern Parkway about twenty minutes later. As the *New York Times* reported under the headline "Brooklyn El Line Dies with Aplomb," the final trip was crowded with railfans and old-time Brooklynites savoring

Taken in January 1951, this photo shows el demolition underway at the three-way intersection of Lexington Avenue, Ralph Avenue, and Broadway. The signal tower is being dismantled. Along Broadway, under the el that carries today's J train, is a whole line of New York mercantile names: F. W. Woolworth's, National Shoes, Loft's candies, and Bohack supermarkets. Schaefer beer, whose truck is making deliveries, is still being brewed, but not in Brooklyn. NYTM

Tompkins Avenue Station, shortly before the end. A then-ubiquitous Burma-Shave advertisement hangs from the platform. NYTM

December 1950. The el is being demolished where it turns from Grand onto Lexington. The customers at Rappaport's luncheonette, right below the el, probably welcomed the end of the noise and vibration, except that many of them probably were also el riders and now had to find alternative routes. NYTM

a final ride on the borough's first elevated route.[1] The celebrants included some Pratt Institute faculty members, who stated that they would enjoy the newly quiet classrooms on their campus, as the Lexington route cut right through the school's grounds.

It is interesting to note that the Lexington Avenue Line connected to both the Myrtle Avenue and Broadway elevated lines, which today are Brooklyn's last remaining nineteenth-century elevated routes. Myrtle's original route joined with the Lexington

1. *New York Times* (October 14, 1950).

line at Grand Avenue. This segment, between Bridge-Jay Streets and Broadway, soldiered on for another nineteen years until it too was closed in October 1969 and razed soon afterward. During that time Myrtle used the oldest rapid transit equipment in New York, hosting late nineteenth-century wooden-gate cars (with open vestibule doors) until 1958, and from then until 1969 using early twentieth-century wooden cars with more modern sliding doors, known as the Q types. The Q types were so-called because the BMT first used them on its Queens routes to Astoria and Flushing. Until October 1969 the Myrtle el hosted two services; the all-elevated original route between Bridge-Jay Streets and Metropolitan Avenue and today's still-operating portion north of Broadway, between Metropolitan Avenue and Manhattan via the Williamsburg Bridge (today's M train). By 1969 the Metropolitan Transportation Authority (MTA) was the umbrella agency in charge of all publicly owned New York City transit lines, and one of its first decisions was to raze the Myrtle line south of Broadway. This route, which also operated near the Pratt Institute campus, had the distinction of being the last rapid transit route in North America to use wooden elevated cars.[2]

BROOKLYN 'EL' LINK DIES WITH APLOMB

Celebrants Pack Last Train to Run on Lexington Spur, Soon to Be Torn Down

IN SERVICE FOR 65 YEARS

Riders Were So Scarce That Its 8 Stations Were Closed at Night for Last 10 Years

Sixty-five years of service ended last night for the Lexington Avenue elevated line, whose eight stations cut through the Bedford-Stuyvesant section of Brooklyn.

The last six-car train started its clattery journey at 9 P. M. Transportation officials, old Brooklyn citizens and "last ride" enthusiasts pushed aboard at the Eastern Parkway station to mark the line's demise as a festive occasion.

The B. M. T.'s oldest motorman and its only remaining qualified locomotive engineman, 69-year-old Christian Earing of 1076 Greene Avenue, Brooklyn, took over the controls for the last ride from the regular motorman, Harry Adams, who went along as passenger.

Mr. Earing's daughter, her husband, and the motorman's two teen-age grandchildren, were along. He has worked on the Lexington line since 1928, and other routes for 52 years. Now he has his choice of any shift until he retires soon. He had finished his regular run on the line that morning.

Wandering through the train, which had four extra cars for the hour when two-car trains usually run, was William C. Anderson, 79 last Monday, oldest passenger and probably the only one who also rode the line in 1885 on the day it opened. He told how, as a 14-year-old pupil at the then P. S. 4, he and his friends got free rides between 3 and 5 P. M. on opening day.

A retired electrical engineer, he came for the ride for "sentiment's sake" but not out of nostalgia.

New York Times (October 14, 1950). The article discusses the previous night's Lexington Avenue el closure.

2. The author of this book was a Pratt Institute graduate student in 1969 when the Myrtle el stopped running.

10

1953–1968: The TA, Tokens, and TWU Triumphant

In 1953 the Board of Transportation was abolished. Its replacement, the New York City Transit Authority (NYCTA), has operated the system since then. In 1968, NYCTA was folded into a much larger New York State authority, the Metropolitan Transportation Authority. This chapter will cover some of the key issues that the NYCTA faced during its fifteen years as an independent agency. Specific events worthy of their own chapters that occurred during this period are covered in Chapters 15 through 20.

The 1948 fare increase to ten cents did not end the Board of Transportation's fiscal woes. Two interim increases occurred—from seven to ten cents for bus fares and from twelve to fifteen cents for combination subway/bus fares on July 1, 1950, and then complete elimination of combination fares on July 1, 1952. These moves did not provide a long-term solution or produce an adequate revenue stream. Ridership was not increasing because of demographic and geographic changes that were beyond the control of the transit system. Increased automobile usage, movement from older inner-city neighborhoods to outlying neighborhoods or newer suburbs, and loss of manufacturing jobs all conspired to reduce demand for traditional rapid transit and surface line services. Labor, material, and energy costs for the transit system continued to rise, and many capital needs of the aging system remained unfunded. An older, unreliable system meant that poor service and crowded trains did not help attract riders. It was a downward spiral. Since the Board of Transportation reported directly to the mayor, the political finger pointing was endless. Mayor LaGuardia's "good deal" of 1940 turned into a fiscal albatross by 1950.

Sixty-plus years later, these issues still sound familiar. Only the dollar amounts have increased. It was clear that another fare increase would be necessary, especially since New York's ten-cent tariff was low compared to other major cities; as an example, Chicago by 1953 had a twenty-cent basic fare after the public Chicago Transit Authority assumed complete control of the Windy City's rapid transit and surface lines. New York's mayor, Board of Estimate, and City Council found that the Board of Transportation was a never-ending political football. A new way to manage and operate the system was needed, one that would create fiscal stability and remove the entire transit system from direct mayoral control.

The public authority was the answer. New York already had two such successful agencies that primarily operated bridges and tunnels for motor traffic—the Port of New York Authority (today's Port Authority of New York and New Jersey) and the Triborough Bridge and Tunnel Authority (TBTA, today's MTA Bridges and Tunnels). TBTA was legally restricted to the five boroughs, so New York State legislation already existed to create another such public authority.

This idea was not new. As noted in Chapter 7 Paul Windels headed a civic group that pushed for years to have the Board of Transportation abolished in favor of an independent agency that could set a realistic fare without political influences. Finally, in March 1953, after much political infighting and compromising, New York State abolished the Board of Transportation and created a new public agency, the New York City Transit Authority (NYCTA), independent of the mayor. By law, NYCTA was required to set fares at a level covering all operating costs, meaning that New York City's operating budget would no longer be used to subsidize mass transit. Capital costs, such as new subway cars, new buses, construction to rehabilitate existing lines and build new ones, and construction of new service and maintenance facilities, would still be funded by the city's capital budget.

The new NYCTA formally succeeded the old Board of Transportation on June 15, 1953. It was composed of five unsalaried members—two appointed by Governor Thomas Dewey (Hugh Casey and Henry K. Norton), two appointed by Mayor Vincent Impellitteri (William Fullen and Ephraim Jeffe), and the fifth appointed by the other four members (Eugene Moran). At the authority's first meeting its members elected Casey as the agency's chairman. The NYCTA then promptly hired the Board of Transportation's former chairman, Sidney H. Bingham, as its new operating chief. At the same time the city government leased the subway and surface system to NYCTA for a ten-year period.

NYCTA's first key decision was the subway fare itself. It had agreed initially not to include a depreciation allowance in its operating cost analysis, which would have put greater pressure on the fare. Mandated to charge a fare sufficient to cover all operating costs, NYCTA increased it to fifteen cents on July 25. Since that fare level eliminated the possibility of a single coin or two of the same coin, a token slightly smaller than a dime was introduced as the medium for paying subway and elevated fares. Bus and trolley fares would continue to be paid in cash only.

When tokens were introduced, it was discovered that play money available in stores at a cost of ten coins for fifteen cents could work in the turnstiles. This issue was corrected two days after the fare increase with an adjustment to the turnstile mechanisms. It helped that Colonel Bingham, the NYCTA general manager, was the nephew of the long-time IRT president Frank Hedley and was instrumental in developing the original subway turnstiles in 1921. Whatever the case, enterprising New Yorkers lost no time

The original sixteen-millimeter token used from 1953 until 1970, for both the fifteen- and twenty-cent fares. www.nycsubway.org

finding new uses for the new tokens. Meyer Berger, the legendary *New York Times* reporter whose column "About New York" was a staple for many years until his untimely 1959 death, noted in his July 29, 1953, column that a diner at a West Side Manhattan coffee shop used a token in lieu of coins for his lunch tip.

Right from the start events occurred that questioned the wisdom of having NYCTA governed by a five-person unsalaried board. Ephraim Jeffe, a mayoral appointee, resigned in July right after the new fifteen-cent fare was announced, in opposition to the new rate. Mayor Impellitteri appointed Harris Klein, a Brooklyn lawyer, to replace Jeffe. Of greater urgency, by the end of November it was noted that the system's ridership had declined by a little over 10 percent since the fare went up. In the context of the twenty-first century a five-cent increase seems like nothing, but in 1953 such an increase, 50 percent over the previous fare, was significant to enough people that many would-be riders were no doubt curtailing nonessential trips.[1] That year, $90 take-home pay per week was considered a good salary. A nickel fare increase for the five-days-a-week regular rider amounted to an increase of fifty cents a week, or about 0.5 percent of that $90. In those days, fifty cents bought a New Yorker two newsstand magazines or a nutted cheese sandwich and cup of coffee at Chock Full o' Nuts.

No one knew it in 1953, but the original fifteen-cent token would itself become worth twenty cents in 1966 and ultimately last until 1970 (when it was replaced by a larger thirty-cent token). Transit tokens, which later appeared after 1970 in different sizes, styles, and values, were a New York icon for fifty years. The final tokens, worth $1.50, were phased out in May 2003, ending a long run that saw electronic fare collection replace old-style coin and token usage.

The NYCTA faced many issues in its fifteen years as an independent agency, and it had its share of challenges and success stories. A key challenge involved labor relations, always a slippery slope, which finally stabilized after years of contentiousness under the old Board of Transportation. Prior to the 1940 subway unification, the Transport Workers Union (TWU) had won the right to represent workers on the IRT, BMT, the city-owned IND subway, and many of the privately owned bus and trolley companies. The TWU was created as an industrial union, using the model of all-encompassing organi-

---

1. *New York Times* (November 23, 1953).

Happy Transport Workers Union officials tallying the votes of the 1954 worker representation election, which gave the TWU exclusive bargaining privileges over all NYCTA hourly workers except those in the Queens and Staten Island bus divisions. The man second from the left pointing at the board is Matthew Guinan, who later would become the international president of the TWU. TWU Local 100 archives

zation representing all workers regardless of job title. This model differed from the older, railroad industry craft model in which each specific job group (craft) has its own representation organization.

Unification and World War II's labor shortages led to a period of unstable and unpredictable labor relations, but the TWU maintained its position as the key bargaining agent for the majority of New York transit workers. Initial moves by Mayor LaGuardia in the early days of unified operations, to declare that a unionized transit work force was illegal on a municipally owned system that gave its workers civil service protection, did not succeed in ending the TWU's hegemony. When World War II ended, costs increased, fares went up, and the city took over additional private bus operators in Staten Island, Queens, and Manhattan (see Chapter 6). In 1949 the TWU and the Board of Transportation, under Mayor William O'Dwyer, signed a Memorandum of Understanding that gave the TWU the right to represent all of the system's workers.

Finally, in 1954 the entire labor representation situation stabilized to the mutual satisfaction of both the TWU and NYCTA. In an NYCTA-wide representation election, the first of its kind, the TWU gained exclusive collective bargaining rights for all NYCTA hourly workers except for Queens and Staten Island Bus Division personnel, who remained with the Amalgamated Association of Street Electric Railway and Motor Coach Employees of America, a holdover from the days when those two divisions were private bus concerns (in 1964 that organization became the Amalgamated Transit Union). The TWU's victory was a plus for the NYCTA's management and for New York City's key transit labor arbitrator, Theodore Kheel. Both the NYCTA and Kheel felt that transit labor relations would be more easily managed if one large union represented the work force instead of a large number of craft-based groups.

However, the TWU's hegemony over most transit workers did not come easily. After the 1954 representation election a series of intraunion skirmishes developed between the TWU hierarchy and craft-based dissident labor groups. The craft groups borrowed from the railroad industry models that predated the TWU. The most outspoken craft unionists were the subway motormen, who often looked at the Brotherhood of Loco-motive Engineers (BLE) on U.S. railroads as their model.[2] A Motormen's Benevolent Association (MBA) was formed in 1954 to further their interests, and in June 1956 a one-day wildcat strike tied up subway service on the BMT division on a ninety-degree day. Having demonstrated their ability to create chaos, the motormen were not about the give up their power of the throttle. The MBA's leadership, including its president, Theodore Loos, were fired after the 1956 strike but were reinstated after they agreed not to strike again.

However, continued efforts to placate the unhappy motormen did not succeed. The-odore Loos was not about to let Mike Quill call all the shots. The motormen were not only the highest-paid operating craft on the subways but also the one group that could literally bring the trains to a standstill in a matter of minutes. Another representation election was scheduled for Monday, December 16, 1957, and the unhappy motormen did not want to continue to be small players in a larger TWU group. The motormen threat-ened to walk out but were thwarted by court injunctions that promised to jail their leadership if any work stoppages occurred.

The motormen wanted to hold their own craft's representation election independent of the overall NYCTA-wide election. The NYCTA management did not recognize the MBA as a bargaining unit because the TWU officially represented the motormen. An overall election virtually guaranteed the TWU's continued power because in that arrangement motormen were just one group of fish in a very large pond of subway conductors, bus drivers, maintenance-of-way workers, mechanics, shop workers, and token clerks, to name a few job titles. Their request for a separate election was denied, and the motor-men's leadership decided that the only way to demonstrate their power and acquire their own representation was to show their power to stop the entire subway system.

So it was on Monday, December 9, 1957, when another wildcat motormen's strike oc-curred, this time with far more serious effects than the previous year. For eight days, subway service was reduced to no more than half of the normal level, with particularly severe impact on the IND lines serving Queens, the Bronx, and Upper Manhattan and on BMT southern Brooklyn lines. Displaced riders were forced onto buses, taxis, Long Island and New York Central commuter trains, and the remaining subway trains that did operate. It was not a pretty sight. One newspaper photo taken the morning of the strike's first day showed a long line of suburban commuters waiting in the rain to board Fifth Avenue Coach Lines Route #4 buses on Fort Washington Avenue, at the foot of the George Washington Bridge. After riding buses from Bergen County (New Jersey) and Rockland County (New York), these riders normally took the A train downtown from the nearby 175th Street Station.

2. In the early twentieth century the BLE tried to organize Brooklyn Rapid Transit motormen.

The *New York Times* of December 10, 1957, shows displaced subway commuters, unable to board their regular trains because of the wildcat subway strike, scrambling for alternative modes in the rain.

Newspaper stories featured people who reached Manhattan from Queens on a combination of local bus trips that consumed half a work day. Extremely heavy traffic at the East River bridges and tunnels, coupled with wet weather, added to the turmoil. Another story noted that one fifty-five-year-old Long Island Rail Road commuter collapsed and died in the human crush at Penn Station trying to reach his homeward train.

Of course, the MBA leaders were punished immediately for violating prior injunctions that prohibited strikes. The first morning of the strike, MBA President Theodore Loos and three other MBA officials were immediately arrested and sent to the Civil Jail on West 37th Street for violating an earlier promise not to strike that stemmed from their 1956 walkout. This would not be the only time a New York transit labor leader would spend some nights in that facility. In 1966 TWU's president Michael Quill was also locked up there after defying a no-strike injunction (Chapter 19 gives more details).

A. H. Raskin, the *New York Times'* distinguished labor writer, wrote a thoughtful analysis of the situation, which he characterized as a revolt of skilled workers submerged in a mass industrial union. According to Raskin, the skilled workers were demanding greater voices in determining their wages and working conditions. One of the byproducts of the TWU's 1954 representation election victory was that "Mr. Quill, once the trumpeting terror of the subway system, has become the darling of the Transit Authority." Quill had been working quietly with the NYCTA to institute work rule efficiencies, part of what Raskin termed a "doctrine of responsibility and industrial stability" versus the old "red meat" diet of confrontation.[3] Now, Quill's problems were within his own union.

In the same edition, the *Times* profiled the MBA's executive secretary, Frank Zelano. A fifty-seven-year-old Brooklyn widower with two teenage daughters, Zelano noted the heavy responsibilities of the motorman's job—a train packed with a thousand or more passengers entering a station with a packed platform, the dangers of persons falling to the tracks, and the constant stress that dangers lurk around every corner. For this, Zelano noted that his take-home base pay was $67 weekly, which he considered too low. He characterized Mike Quill as not giving "a damn about motormen" and only caring about "sweetheart contracts" with NYCTA management.[4]

After the fourth day the striking motormen offered to meet directly with Mayor Robert Wagner to work out a peace plan and get service back to normal. Wagner proposed that the striking motormen not be dismissed but that each individual case be decided by an impartial referee that he would appoint. The TWU was also urged to consider the specific grievances unique to motormen.

The strike continued, with subway service improving after the third day but not back to normal until December 16. Mayor Wagner finally restored full subway service on that date when he warned the dissident motormen that if they did not return their jobs would be in jeopardy.

In 1958, the TWU and the MBA reached a settlement. The motormen became a separate United Motormen's Division within the TWU and benefitted from a special $2.5 million fund established for skilled craft workers.[5] Theodore Loos became its head; Frank Zelano continued to press for a separate bargaining unit and eventually lost his job. There was never a significant craft-based work stoppage on the subways after this event, as the TWU became the single, undisputed bargaining agent for all NYCTA hourly paid employees except those working for the Queens and Staten Island Bus Divisions, whose workers, to this day, are represented by the Amalgamated Transit Union.

Viewed in retrospect in the twenty-first century, the 1954 TWU victory was a win-win for TA management and industrial-model labor and a personal victory for TWU President Mike Quill and the labor mediator Theodore Kheel. Quill always preached the benefits of industry-wide industrial unionism versus individual craft organizations; Kheel always felt that dealing with one large union made his job easier. This pattern was in contrast to the craft union approach of the American Federation of Labor, which believed that workers should be organized by individual craft, not by industry. This was the model used in the railroad field, where unions developed representing many different workers—for example, engineers, conductors, track workers, signal

3. *New York Times* (December 11, 1957).
4. *New York Times* (December 11, 1957).
5. Joshua B. Freeman, *In Transit* (New York: Oxford University Press, 1989), 332.

workers. The rationale for an industry-wide union, from the TWU standpoint, was historical. The private transit companies that preceded NYCTA treated their work forces so shabbily that the only way that organized labor could be effective in that environment was to organize everyone on a global scale, so that managements could not practice a divide-and-conquer technique in order to reduce the effectiveness of any union.

It also helped that Mayor Robert F. Wagner, who served from 1954 through 1965, was well regarded in the labor movement, since he was the son of the famous U.S. senator who championed prolabor legislation during the New Deal era. The younger Wagner also encouraged the growth of municipal worker unions beyond the TWU, and the union considered Wagner an ally. In 1958 he formally signed city legislation that allowed municipal workers to join unions and bargain collectively, a law known as the "Little Wagner Act." Spurred by the TWU's experience, other key city workers, such as police, firefighters, and schoolteachers, all became unionized in the ensuring few years.

One provision in the 1953 law that created NYCTA mandated that by July 1955 the agency develop a specific plan to sell its bus and trolley routes to private operators, although no deadline for the actual sale was in the law. As reported in early 1955, the authority's surface operations, comprising bus-only divisions in Manhattan, Queens, and Staten Island and a bus and trolley division in Brooklyn, was costing seven million dollars more to operate annually than it collected in fare revenue.[6] It was felt that by privatizing (to use a contemporary term) these services and concentrating on subways, NYCTA could meet all of its operating costs.

In March 1955 two Manhattan private bus operators, New York City Omnibus and Surface Transportation, did express interest in taking over the five-route NYCTA network in that borough.[7] Omnibus asked to buy the 49th–50th and Madison–Chambers Streets crosstown routes, while Surface tried to obtain the York Avenue, First–Second Avenue, and 65th–66th Street crosstown routes. While there was reported interest in some Queens routes from existing private operators in that borough, there was little or no interest in the Brooklyn and Staten Island networks. Brooklyn was a huge undertaking, by itself bigger than many whole city bus networks, and it still included a few streetcar and trolley coach routes. Staten Island's long route distances and relatively light ridership caused those routes to be perpetual money losers and unattractive to any potential private buyers. The issue died fairly quickly because effective July 1, 1955, New York State law created a new, three-person, salaried Transit Authority that replaced the original 1953 five-person body. The mandated plan to sell the bus and trolley routes was quietly removed from the law creating the three-person Transit Authority.[8]

6. *New York Times* (February 7, 1955).
7. *New York Times* (March 28, 1955).
8. *New York Times* (June 17, 1955).

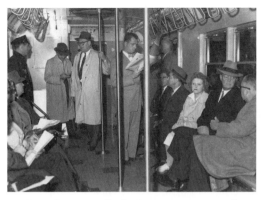

NYCTA Chairman Charles Patterson is pictured riding a then-new BMT R27 car in November 1960. He's the man standing and wearing a light raincoat and dark fedora. NYTM

Chairman Patterson tries out a new IRT R28 car, about 1961. This time he is not mingling anonymously with customers. NYTM

Exterior shot of a brand-new R27 consist at Coney Island Yard, early 1961. The train is signed for the QT Brighton–Broadway–Forest Hills Local. Later that year the QT was reassigned to serve Astoria, and RR trains took over the Forest Hills route. NYTM

An R21 IRT car on the #1 Broadway Line, part of a 1957 order for 250 such cars from St. Louis Car Company. It is shown about 1958, at the 240th Street Yard in the Bronx. Its destination is New Lots Avenue, Brooklyn, which was the #1's south terminal before the February 1959 service change that switched all #1 trains to South Ferry via the local tracks. NYTM

Chairman Patterson and St. Louis Car Company head Edwin Meissner, signing a contract for that firm to provide new subway cars to New York, about 1960. Meissner's firm built 3850 NYCTA cars between 1955 and 1969. NYTM

A group of brand-new IRT R29 cars make a triumphant entrance into the city they will serve, sailing under the Brooklyn Bridge in March 28, 1962. NYTM

Interior of a new R29 car, assigned to the #1 Broadway Local route, in 1962. NYTM

As things turned out long term, no private operators ever took over any NYCTA bus routes, with the single exception of the Q72 Junction Boulevard line in Queens, which in 1961 was transferred from NYCTA to Triboro Coach Corporation. Instead, two large public takeovers of the private bus networks ultimately did occur, one in 1962 (Fifth Avenue Coach/Surface Transit, covered in Chapter 17), and one forty-plus years later (2005–2006), when the Metropolitan Transportation Authority took over the remaining private operators in the Bronx, Brooklyn, and Queens. A small Manhattan operator, Avenue B and East Broadway Transit, sold out to NYCTA in 1980.

NYCTA itself changed after its second year. Its five-person, unsalaried board was recognized as ineffective because its members could not devote their full time to managing the transit system. The New York State legislature passed laws in April 1955 that changed the NYCTA, effective July 1, 1955, to a three-member salaried panel, whose members were mandated to devote their full time to the subways and buses. Joseph O'Grady and Vincent Curtayne were appointed by Mayor Robert Wagner and Governor Averill Harriman respectively. In turn they chose as the new chairman a lifelong railroad executive, Charles Patterson, a Pittsburgh native who had worked for the Pennsylvania, Bessemer and Lake Erie, Long Island, and Lehigh Valley Railroads.

During the TA's fifteen-year independent tenure, it put into service large numbers of new cars to replace equipment that dated from as early as 1914. The biggest problem about the system it inherited in 1953 was the age of both IRT and BMT car fleets, something that Patterson strove to change as soon as he became chairman. When the IND subway opened in 1932, the Board of Transportation began using the designation "R," plus a number, to identify every new rapid transit car order. The IND subway's cars delivered between 1931 and 1941 were designated R1 through R9. Between 1947 and 1950 the IRT received its first large car order since the 1920s, when the R12, R14, and R15 series cars were delivered, featuring fluorescent lighting and double-leaf doors. The IND received its first postwar equipment in 1948 when the R10 series debuted; it was an IND-size version of the IRT's R12. An experimental group of ten stainless steel cars built to IND dimensions, the R11 series, came in 1949 but were not successful.

After NYCTA replaced the Board of Transportation, its new cars first appeared in January 1955 when two hundred R16 models, designed for BMT and IND routes, were put in service on the Broadway/Brooklyn–Jamaica Avenue Elevated (today's J train). These cars were the first New York rolling stock equipped with automatic thermostats and dampers to control the heating and ventilating systems based on the outside air temperature. Additional car orders for the BMT/IND types R27-30 and R32 came in service between 1960 and 1964 and totaled 1,150 units. Between 1966 and 1969, another thousand cars of the R38, R40, and R42 classes were ordered and placed in service, for a grand total of 2,350 new cars for the combined BMT-IND services. All retained the basic design envelope of the original IND R1 car—sixty feet in length with four doors per side.

The IRT had even more pressing needs to replace obsolete stock, resulting in orders for R17, R21, R22, R26, R28, R29, R33, and R36 units totaling 2,510 units between 1955 and 1964. The grand total of 4,860 new units the NYCTA ordered between 1953 and 1968 represented about two-thirds of the total fleet size of 6,500 units. These cars, now themselves all out of service except for about two hundred R32 and fifty R42 units, went a long way toward giving the system a more modern appearance. The cars introduced fluorescent lighting, dynamic braking, and roller bearings to the car fleet. Air conditioning, now a universal feature, did not appear until the last two hundred of the four-hundred-car R40 order came so equipped. This feature was the culmination of many years of experimentation and research on earlier cars, including ten R38 cars built in 1967 that proved the viability of subway air conditioning. Later, many of the cars in these individual orders would be retrofitted with air conditioning. Chapter 18 goes into more detail about two car specific car classes, the R32 and R36.

New cars were the most visible improvement made to the subway system during the 1953–1968 period, but not the only one. Route expansions also occurred, although not nearly as extensive as the new authority envisioned initially. In July 1953 NYCTA proposed capital spending totaling $1,065,000,000 over six years, expanding subway operations by a combination of new lines and connections between existing IND and BMT routes. Key new lines were a Second Avenue subway (including a Chrystie Street connection to the Manhattan Bridge and a rebuilt DeKalb Avenue junction in Brooklyn), IRT Nostrand and Utica Avenue extensions into southeastern Brooklyn, and extension of subway service to the Rockaway Peninsula using a Long Island Rail Road branch.[9] The Rockaway Line, the IND-BMT connections, the DeKalb Avenue recon-

9. *New York Times* (July 24, 1953).

In late 1959 NYCTA put in service the first New Look GMC buses, a radical design change from the firm's previous buses. They were unofficially dubbed "fishbowls" because of their large front windshield. On October 19, 1959, five of the new vehicles were displayed outside City Hall, to the obvious delight of the smartly uniformed driver outside the bus on the right. NYTM

Interior of an early 1960s NYCTA "fishbowl" bus. The front half's seats were longitudinal in order to open up the front half and make it easy for passengers to reach the rear transverse seats. This arrangement was used until 1965, when buses were equipped entirely with longitudinal seats. NYTM

It's August 1962, and etiquette maven Amy Vanderbilt is shown on a NYCTA "fishbowl" bus in Manhattan, about to embark on a month-long series of rides to develop a conduct manual for drivers and passengers. The veteran TV reporter Gabe Pressman is at left. NYTM

In the 1960s, long before the word Metrocard had even been dreamed up, there were only two locations citywide where a free transfer between a subway and bus were permitted. One was at Rockaway Parkway Station at the end of the BMT Canarsie Line, where the B42 bus drove into a separate paid area adjacent to the platform. NYTM

struction, and the Chrystie Street connection were built between 1954 and 1967. Chapter 12 and Chapter 19 describe these projects in more detail. But the actual Second Avenue Subway north of Chrystie Street (with connections to the Bronx and Queens) and the two IRT extensions in Brooklyn were not built, although the former is indeed now nearly completed between 63rd and 96th Streets. Much debate occurred in the 1950s and 1960s over the Transit Authority's decision to spend the majority of capital funds

The last NYCTA buses purchased prior to the MTA's creation were 682 of this model, a GMC TDH 5303A delivered in 1967. An updated version of the "fishbowl" bus, this one is on the B41/Flatbush Avenue route in Brooklyn. The blank space in the large sign above the windows would soon be sold to advertisers. Buses in this group were the first in the NYCTA to have air conditioning. NYTM

In January 1955, Miss Subways Phyllis Johnson, a U.S. Army officer, tried out a new BMT R16 car on the Broadway–Brooklyn–Jamaica Avenue Line (today's J train). NYTM

to upgrade existing routes instead of building new ones. It is now recognized that it was wiser to concentrate on the existing routes.

On the bus side, NYCTA introduced the first U.S. transit buses with fiberglass seating in 1957, as a way to combat seat cushion vandalism; the same year buses came equipped with push-out rear doors that the passenger controlled. In 1960 NYCTA introduced its first "New Look" or "Fishbowl" buses, which then represented a radical change from the 1940s/1950s styles that were ubiquitous up to that time. Since General Motors emerged by then as the preeminent U.S. transit bus builder and had only one domestic competitor after 1960, it was no surprise that NYCTA was a major GM customer. The "fishbowl" moniker referred to the bus's large front window. NYCTA's fishbowl buses until 1966 had a unique seating arrangement that had longitudinal seating in the front and transverse seating beyond the rear door, the idea being that the front of the bus would be opened up and induce passengers to move to the rear seating. After 1966 buses came equipped with completely longitudinal seating as a means of maximizing standing room. The following year saw the first air-conditioned buses, a promise that John Lindsay made when he became mayor the previous year, a development that certainly made travel more comfortable.

Speaking of comfortable bus travel, in August 1962 NYCTA announced with some fanfare that it had hired Amy Vanderbilt, the etiquette maven, to ride its buses for a

February 1962 ceremony at the Queens Boulevard IND subway line's 67th Avenue Station in Forest Hills. Residential growth in this neighborhood required the opening of new street stairways plus a second token booth and turnstiles. The tall man in the middle is Queens Borough President John T. Clancy. NYTM

In 1960 and 1961 New York Titans football fans could travel between Queens and the Polo Grounds on a special fifty-cent fare game-day train that operated directly between the Queens IND at 179th Street/Jamaica and 155th Street in Manhattan. The Titans, of course, became the Jets in 1963. NYTM

month-long period in order to create a list of courtesy rules for passengers and drivers. Vanderbilt agreed to do this work without charge. As The *New York Times* noted with some sarcasm in its August 22 edition, "There have been ugly rumors that New York bus drivers and their passengers do not always exchange pleasantries." The day before, Vanderbilt had kicked off her project on a NYCTA bus at 47th Street and First Avenue. Unfortunately there is no surviving record of the results of her courtesy campaign.

While on the subject of female personalities and the NYCTA, the agency continued to run its bimonthly Miss Subways contest until 1976. The winners came from many different backgrounds. In January 1955, Phyllis Johnson, a U.S. Army officer, was photographed on a new R16 car as it made its inaugural run.

By the mid-1960s, the NYCTA had reversed the downward spiral in transit riding largely because the fifteen-cent fare was perceived as a good value while other consumer goods and services witnessed price increases. The large numbers of new cars placed in service after 1955 also helped. Even minor events, such as the opening of new entrances at the Forest Hills, Queens, subway station, were publicized in order for NYCTA to remind New Yorkers that it was striving to improve the transit system in big and small ways.

Speaking of Queens subways, in the fall of 1960 and again in 1961 NYCTA and the city's new American Football League franchise (the Titans, now the Jets) teamed up to operate a long-forgotten special subway train between the IND Queens Line and the Polo Grounds to accommodate fans. A special train departed from 179th Street and Hillside Avenue about ninety minutes before the game, and after arriving at 42nd Street and Eighth Avenue and making its only stop reversed direction and traveled uptown to 155th Street and Eighth Avenue. A special fifty-cent fare was charged, collected using a special ticket. Once arrived at the game a fan could use the ticket to pay for part of the cost of a grandstand seat. No such arrangement was ever provided for the National Football League's Giants, which then played home games at Yankee Stadium.

Unfortunately Chairman Charles Patterson would not be around to see many fruits of his labors. The often stubborn and colorful Patterson, a classic railroad boss, died on October 13, 1962, at the age of fifty-six. One of his key projects, the 59th Street lower-level express stop on the Lexington Avenue subway, opened a month later. This work, part of a reconstruction package that modernized the entire Lexington Avenue route between 125th Street and Bowling Green, involved building a brand new express station on the bottom level of a triple-decked tunnel structure.

The fifteen years in which the New York City Transit Authority was its own agency, prior to the MTA's creation in 1968, should be remembered as a positive time if for no other reason than that only a single fare increase occurred in that time. Indeed, the fifteen-cent fare remained in effect until from July 25, 1953, until July 5, 1966, when it went up to twenty cents, where it remained until January 1970. So for nearly seventeen years New York's fare was either fifteen or twenty cents. Those tariffs were lower than most other large U.S. cities at the time. Chicago's twenty-five-cent base fare was increased to thirty cents in 1967 and forty cents in 1969; Philadelphia's twenty-five-cent base went to thirty cents in 1968. By then the only large U.S. cities with fares lower than New York were San Francisco (fifteen cents) and New Orleans (ten cents). The former was the first U.S. city to own and operate its own transit system (1912); the latter was the last large U.S. city system to remain in private hands (until 1983). The common thread in New York, San Francisco, and New Orleans was the high percentages of each city's residents who were regular transit riders.

Another memorable mid-1960s event was the Great Northeast Blackout on November 9, 1965. On that moonlit Tuesday night, the electric power grid all over the northeastern United States failed just after 5 PM. In New York the juice dried up at 5:27 PM, at the height of the homeward rush hour. On the subways, eight hundred thousand customers on six hundred trains were marooned in dark tunnels, on elevated structures, and on bridges. By midnight all but ten thousand had been escorted safely out of the system; those passengers were sent food before they were taken off their trains. The last passengers evacuated were on an Astoria-bound BMT trip who elected to stay with their train, deep under the East River, until power was restored. The most difficult evacuation occurred on the Williamsburg Bridge, where 1,700 passengers on four trains were slowly escorted to the Brooklyn or Manhattan sides. They had to walk sin-

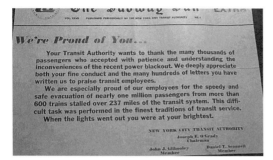

Subway Sun poster from November 1965, thanking subway passengers for their calm behavior during the power blackout that month. www.thejoekorner.com

New York Times (November 11, 1965), two days after the power blackout.

gle file on narrow catwalks until they could access the bridge's roadway, and it took five hours to clear the four trains.[10]

Buses continued to run, naturally with great difficulty. Lack of traffic signals and streetlights was a major safety hazard. Displaced subway passengers quickly over-whelmed the available buses, particularly where bus routes operated parallel to rapid transit. The photo from the *New York Times* article is not an exaggeration—it shows a northbound M10 bus on Manhattan's Eighth Avenue after the blackout occurred. De-spite these daunting circumstances, there was no panic and only one minor injury. The NYCTA placed posters on the trains a few days later thanking its customers for their heroism during the power emergency.

Fifty-two days after the blackout was over, the subways faced a greater crisis, perhaps the greatest up to that time. January 1, 1966, the trains and buses stopped for twelve days, during the first citywide transit strike. Chapter 19 will cover this event in detail.

Despite the successes of the 1953–1968 period, external pressures both political and economic worked to push NYCTA into a larger public agency—the Metropolitan Transportation Authority—in 1968. This event will be covered in Chapter 20.

10. *New York Times* (November 11, 1965).

11

1953: Last Double-Deck Buses Operate on Fifth Avenue

Fifth Avenue Coach Company, as noted in Chapter 2, was famous for the double-deck buses it operated on its namesake thoroughfare and on connecting streets and avenues in Upper Manhattan and Queens. After the 1941 strike was settled, one contentious labor issue that festered throughout the World War II years was two-man operation on Fifth Avenue's double-deck buses. From the beginnings of the operation in 1907, two-man crews—driver and conductor—were standard on the double deckers. Conductors collected fares and controlled passenger movement on and off the bus; the driver simply operated the vehicle.

Even before the war started, the company management was making arguments that double deckers, particularly the newer Queen Mary models with their front entrances, could be operated by one man.[1] The company's annual reports noted that their corporate cousin, Chicago Motor Coach, and the Philadelphia Transportation Company operated one-man double deckers. The TWU naturally opposed this proposal, wanting to protect its members' jobs. The management did not intend simply to fire the conductors; rather, it proposed to retrain conductors under sixty years of age to become bus operators on its affiliate NYC Omnibus. Conductors over sixty would be retired on lifetime pensions; those under sixty and not trainable as bus drivers would still be retained in light-duty jobs.

The dispute dragged on for years, with the company threatening simply to replace all double deckers with single-deck coaches that under the labor agreements used a driver only. In December 1946, after the war ended, the conductor dispute was finally resolved when the last pre-1936 double-deck buses were retired. As was noted in Fifth Avenue's 1946 annual report, "The long debate over the use of conductors on double deck buses was resolved, with the institution of one man operation in December 1946

---

1. The Queen Mary double deckers were given that unofficial moniker because 1936 was the same year that the Cunard ocean liner *Queen Mary* began operating between New York and Great Britain. General Motors (Yellow Truck and Coach Division) built 160 of these buses for Fifth Avenue Coach between 1936 and 1938, in two different model configurations—sixty model 720s and one hundred model 735s. The 720 had a roofline six inches lower (12 feet 6 inches versus 13 feet on the 735s) to enable it to operate on the #15 Jackson Heights route, which had restricted overhead clearances on the Queensboro Bridge and under the Flushing Line elevated structure along Roosevelt Avenue.

Three double-deckers, led by #2060, are operating southbound on Fifth Avenue, stopping at the 42nd Street Library, about 1950. NYTM

#2029, a model 735 Yellow Coach, has completed an uptown run on route 5 and is laying over at 168th Street and Broadway, opposite the Columbia-Presbyterian Medical Center. The bus will soon turn around to head south, as the destination sign already notes. Motor Bus Society

#2115 is on a northbound route 5 trip on 135th Street between Riverside Drive and Broadway, about 1951. Motor Bus Society

#2429, a GMC 4509, is at 167th Street and Broadway on a route 5 trip to Wanamaker Terminal (9th Street and Broadway) in 1953. Motor Bus Society

under extremely adverse conditions." The 160 Queen Mary coaches became one-man operated and were assigned only to routes 2, 5, and 15. A new group of 157 GM single-deck, forty-four-passenger, thirty-five-foot buses (models TDH-4506 and 4507) were placed in service in 1946 and 1947 on routes 1, 3, 4, and 19. Prewar Yellow 740 single-deck buses ran on crosstown routes 6, 16, and 20. The drivers on the double-deck routes were paid ten cents an hour more than their single-deck counterparts.

And adverse conditions indeed they were. As reported in the *New York Times* a few days after the changeover to one-man buses, drivers complained of slow loading, the additional responsibility of fare collection and change making, and the additional loads given the timing of the changeover during the pre-Christmas shopping rush.

#2498, a Mack C50 that replaced the double deckers on route 15, is shown on Roosevelt Avenue in Jackson Heights, about 1954. Motor Bus Society

#2519, a GMC 5104 that replaced the last Fifth Avenue Coach double-deckers on Riverside Drive, is shown on route 5 in a posed shot near Grant's Tomb about 1953. Motor Bus Society

#2320, a GMC 4507, is finishing a southbound route 5 trip as it enters Washington Square in the mid-1950s. Motor Bus Society

In 1950, #2501, a GMC 5102, and a Yellow Coach double-decker are shown in 1950 in Jackson Heights handling route 15 assignments. Motor Bus Society

The long-term reason for the conversion to one-man buses was an earlier decision by Fifth Avenue's management, under the guidance of its corporate parents in Chicago, not to invest in new double-deck buses once the Queen Mary fleet reached the end of its useful life. While the double deckers were indeed famous, they were slow to load and unload because of the narrow stairs that provided the only access to and from the upper salon. The buses themselves were slow to accelerate because of their heavy weight, and they had to be carefully routed to avoid vertical obstructions.

In an effort to create a single-deck bus that could be a replacement for both New York and Chicago double-deckers and streetcars in all U.S. cities, in 1940 Yellow Coach built an experimental, 41.5-foot single-deck coach, model 5401, with fifty-four seats. At the time the largest single-deck buses were thirty-five feet long with forty-four seats. The bus was sent to Fifth Avenue in 1942, was given fleet number 2500, and ran on the #15 Jackson Heights route until 1946. Returned to Detroit for rebuilding to forty feet long so it would legal everywhere, it was returned to New York in 1948. After being lent to the New York City Board of Transportation for experimental runs in Brooklyn,

Queens, and Staten Island, #2500 then returned to Fifth Avenue Coach and was purchased outright. It ran on the #15 Jackson Heights route until 1962 and was afterward transferred to routes in Westchester County where it ran until it was destroyed in a 1968 garage fire. While it and a similar unique bus (Fifth Avenue fleet #2501) were never duplicated, #2500 was indeed the precursor of the standard forty-foot GM urban transit coach that dominated service in U.S. cities well into the 1960s.

Additional forty-four-passenger GM buses, seventy-four new model 4509s with the newer paired side windows, were delivered in 1950. Beginning in 1951, the Queen Marys ran their final miles and were replaced by forty-foot, fifty-passenger buses that were now available from the major manufacturers. With the exception of two White Motor Company demonstrators purchased in 1938, Fifth Avenue and NYC Omnibus had purchased every bus in their fleets, totaling nearly two thousand vehicles, from Yellow Coach or General Motors between 1935 and 1951. That year, the mold was broken when a fleet of twenty-five Mack Corporation model C50 buses were placed in service on the #15 Jackson Heights route, replacing the model 720 Queen Marys. The #5 Riverside Drive route was the final assignment for the remaining Queen Marys, and the last one ran on April 27, 1953. Afterward, a fleet of fifty GM model 5104 forty-foot, forty-nine-passenger buses became the mainstays on Riverside Drive, along with a mixed group of forty-four-passenger 4506s, 4507s, and 4509s.

The end of the double-decker bus runs was almost unnoticed in the media, despite that the two-level buses were an iconic symbol of Fifth Avenue itself for nearly fifty years. The event also was the very last operation of double-deck urban transit buses in any U.S. city, ending a historic era in the transit history. Philadelphia Transportation Company had stopped such service at the end of World War II, and Chicago Motor Coach, Fifth Avenue's corporate cousin, ran its last Queen Marys in 1950.

12

1954–1956: The BMT and IND Begin a Courtship

In March 1925 construction began on the IND subway system with a ground breaking at 123rd Street and St. Nicholas Avenue in Manhattan. Prior to this event, the IND's engineers deliberately decided to make the new system physically compatible with the older BMT subway, the idea being that, in the future, should the BMT be recaptured by the City of New York, track connections could be built between the IND and BMT that would indeed permit trains to use both systems. One key IND route in Brooklyn—the Fulton Street subway—was even built directly below the older BMT Fulton Street Elevated with the thought of replacing the elevated if the city should ever buy out the BMT. A second IND route, the Prospect Park branch to Church and McDonald Avenues, was designed for easy extension onto the BMT's Culver Line elevated route south of the Church Avenue Station.

In retrospect, the decision to make the IND match BMT dimensions was a wise decision that allowed necessary changes to subway routings in later years.

After unification occurred in June 1940 construction began on a ramp extension of the IND subway south of its terminal at Church and McDonald Avenues that would allow trains to continue south all the way to Coney Island, replacing BMT trains on the Culver Line elevated route (referred to herein as the Culver Connection). Even before World War II began in December 1941, this ramp was left unfinished along with a large group of other key municipal capital projects, as steel and other construction materials were diverted to help the war effort of America's European allies.[1]

With the war's end, the Board of Transportation once again began planning for a modern postwar subway system that would permit the operational advantages of a combined BMT and IND network. On December 15, 1947, the *New York Times* published a lengthy article detailing plans for a massive postwar subway expansion. The key new line was the six-track Second Avenue subway, stretching between the Manhattan Bridge (Chrystie and Canal Streets) and 149th Street/Third Avenue. It would be linked to a variety of existing routes in Manhattan and the Bronx, and its usefulness would be justified by construction of a number of smaller links between IND

---

1. *New York Times* (August 18, 1941).

New York Times (December 15, 1947).

and BMT routes—one in Brooklyn, one in Queens, and one on the Brooklyn-Queens border.

Board of Transportation reports that were published in 1949 and again in 1951 highlighted the Second Avenue subway as the nucleus of a large number of planned subway construction projects designed to improve service in all four subway boroughs. In the twenty-first century, the Second Avenue subway is finally under construction, but three of the smaller links envisioned in 1947 were actually completed between 1954 and 1956 and are still in everyday use.

The first of these links was the aforementioned Culver Connection in Brooklyn's Kensington neighborhood. It was relatively simple in scope and design. A ramp connected the IND Church Avenue Station, then the D train's south terminus, to the BMT Culver Line's Ditmas Avenue Station, without any intermediate stops added. IND trains would then provide through service all the way to Coney Island, replacing the BMT Culver route and creating additional capacity on other BMT routes in southern Brooklyn— the Brighton, Sea Beach, West End, and Fourth Avenue trains. The BMT Culver Line was physically severed from its old route south of Ditmas Avenue and operated only between there and Chambers Street in Lower Manhattan. The resulting low ridership because of the new IND service caused the BMT Culver route to become, in May 1959, a four-station shuttle between Ninth Avenue/36th Street and Ditmas Avenue.

Besides the ramp itself two additional key construction pieces were needed. First, all Culver Line station platforms from Ditmas Avenue to Coney Island were lengthened to

Looking north from the northbound Ditmas Avenue platform, October 1950. The future link to the IND is in place but has only one track installed. All trains are BMT and will turn left onto 39th Street. NYTM

Construction underway in May 1953 to add a fourth track to the southbound side at Ditmas Avenue to allow BMT shuttle trains to terminate there after the IND connection is completed. PCC on the #50/ McDonald route is visible at far right. Billboard ads are for Park and Telford whiskey ($4.02) and Mounds and Almond Joy candies. NYTM

May 1953 construction is underway on the southbound side to relocate a stairway. NYTM

It's August 1953, and construction of the new shuttle track is finished. A PCC car on the #50/McDonald route is visible behind a sign that says "Caution Trolley Turn." NYTM

610 feet to accommodate ten-car IND trains. Second, the Ditmas Avenue Station was extensively rebuilt to provide a single-track stub terminal for the now greatly shortened BMT service. A fourth track was added to the elevated structure on the Coney Island–bound side, including a cross-platform transfer between southbound trains. Northbound passengers from Coney Island would need to use a crossover between the two platforms to transfer between IND and BMT trains. This work was completed in October 1954, and IND D trains began using the new, extended routing on the 30th of that month. The D route now connected 205th Street in the Bronx with Brooklyn's southern shore.

This service change was noteworthy for a number of reasons. It marked the first time the IND division's service invaded the BMT's previously exclusive territory in southern Brooklyn and the first time that a person could ride one train without chang-

It's October 1961; the Ditmas Avenue station has been part of the IND for seven years. The view of the northbound platform shows a sign directing passengers wishing to transfer to BMT trains. Ads to the right of the station sign are for Ronzoni spaghetti sauce, Dick Tracy cartoons on Channel 11, and Aqueduct Race Track. NYTM

Ditmas Avenue about 1974, twenty years after the Culver Connection was opened. The train on the left is an R44 consist on the F line; on the right is an R27-30 consist on the Culver Shuttle, by then called the "SS" route (on maps, anyway). In 1975 the Culver Shuttle ended. NYTM

ing between Coney Island and Upper Manhattan and the Bronx. This one-seat ride also became, at the time, the longest single train ride on the system, about twenty-six miles. (Later the A train between 207th Street and Far Rockaway broke the D train's record.) It also meant that the R1-9 cars assigned to the D train were fitted with windshield wipers, formerly not needed as these cars had spent virtually their entire trips underground (exceptions being the Smith Street Viaduct and the temporary World's Fair Line in 1939–1940).

Finally, in a city where subway route changes are often expected every few years, the Culver Line elevated route has only seen one significant modification since 1954. In November 1967, when the Chrystie Street connection opened (Chapter 20), F trains originating from 179th Street–Jamaica replaced D trains and continue to serve the line today. For a few years some F trains operated express during rush hours between Church Avenue and Kings Highway, but that service has since been dropped. More recently, there have been instances when G trains provided weekend service along the Culver Line during scheduled maintenance work that prevented normal F service. In May 1975 the post-1959 Culver Shuttle between Ditmas and Ninth Avenues was eliminated completely and the old el structure along 39th Street ultimately removed.

The following year another short link was completed. Construction had begun in 1950 on the Eleventh Street Connection, named for the street it follows in Long Island City, Queens. Its purpose was to connect the BMT's 60th Street Tunnel, which had unused train capacity, with the IND Queens Boulevard local tracks just west of Queens

December 1, 1955, ribbon cutting that inaugurated BMT-IND local service via the 60th Street Tunnel and the Queens Boulevard subway. Location is the Queens Plaza IND station. The young lady cutting the ribbon, from the front of a BMT Standard car, is Miss Subways Marie Leonard. Flanking her are TA Chairman Charles Patterson (left) and Leonard's father, TA car inspector Frank Leonard. www.thejoekorner.com

The same location after the ribbon cutting, aboard the BMT Standard car. NYTM

Plaza Station.[2] When the IND Queens Boulevard line opened in 1937, express trains originating at 169th Street or Parsons Boulevard (first E and after 1940 F trains as well) only stopped at Roosevelt Avenue and Queens Plaza south of Forest Hills–71st Avenue. Local trains that turned at Forest Hills served all intermediate stations up to Queens Plaza, but because these locals were GG Brooklyn/Queens crosstown trains, passengers traveling between Manhattan and any local station between Queens Plaza and Forest Hills had to change trains at Queens Plaza or Roosevelt Avenue. Not only was this an inconvenience, but in the rush hours it exacerbated the crowding on the E and F trains.

Fortunately there was a solution—the Eleventh Street Connection. This short, two-track, completely underground piece of construction opened on December 1, 1955, after

2. In subway parlance, this location is operationally south of Queens Plaza because trains leaving Queens are operating toward Lower Manhattan and Brooklyn.

It's April 1942, and a temporary roadway is being built at Pitkin Avenue and Doscher Street to facilitate construction of the IND subway extension directly under the BMT Fulton el, while the el trains continue to run. Chestnut Street Station is at top right. This location is just west of today's underground Euclid Avenue Station, opened in November 1948. NYTM

Also in April 1942, work continues on the new subway under Pitkin Avenue as the old el turns north onto Euclid Avenue on its one-block jog to Liberty Avenue. This location is near the Brooklyn-Queens border, known to old-timers as City Line. NYTM

It's May 1942, and the subway structure is being built below Pitkin Avenue's intersection with Conduit Blvd. (then Sunrise Highway), in the City Line neighborhood at the Brooklyn-Queens border. Wood planking will be used to cover the excavation during construction. NYTM

It's April 1945, and work continues on the new subway at the intersection of Atkins and Pitkin Avenues in East New York. NYTM

nearly five years of construction. It connected the Broadway BMT's 60th Street Tunnel, then operating at about two-thirds of its capacity, with the Queens Boulevard IND local tracks at Queens Plaza. The new connection permitted ten more trains per hour to operate between Manhattan and Queens. Customers who lived in the vicinities of local stations between 36th Street and 67th Avenue had direct one-seat subway service to the heart of Manhattan. No longer would Queens Boulevard local passengers be forced to use overcrowded E and F express trains to access Manhattan.

When BMT trains began running to Forest Hills, it marked the first time that its sixty-seven-foot Standard Cars operated on an IND route. The Brooklyn Rapid Transit Company, BMT's corporate predecessor, designed the Standard Car in 1914 to provide

It's November 1945, and underground construction continues on Pitkin Avenue between Atkins and Montauk. Temporary supports are being put place for the el. NYTM

Early 1950s at Pitkin and Montauk Avenues, with the BMT el station above and still in service. As is so common in New York neighborhoods, small local businesses dot the corners: a tavern, luncheonette, and department store. NYTM

Euclid Avenue Station's mezzanine, about 1956, soon after subway service began to and from the Rockaways. A large floor sign telling passengers about the new services is partly visible in the middle of the photo, to the left of a trash receptacle. NYTM

Rockaway Blvd. Station in June 1955, just before work to lengthen the two platforms would begin. On the left is the Manhattan-bound (northbound) platform. NYTM

service on its new subway routes built under the Dual Contracts. These cars ran on all BMT Dual Contracts routes but had never ventured onto IND tracks until 1955, though the opposite had occurred twice before. In 1931 then-new IND R1 cars were tested in revenue service on the BMT Sea Beach Express, and in the late 1940s and early 1950s, when some R1-9 cars were assigned to the BMT Fourth Avenue Local to alleviate BMT equipment shortages. Along with the Culver Line becoming an IND service in 1954, BMT Standards on Queens Boulevard was another example of the good results of the original decision to make the IND compatible with the BMT.

The new BMT Queens Boulevard service was operated weekdays only between roughly 6 AM and 7 PM. It did not become a 24/7 route until 1987. Unlike its Culver Line cousin, the hybrid BMT-IND Broadway–Queens Boulevard line has hosted a multitude of train routes and route designations over the years. Initially, Brighton Local trains provided service. In 1961, Fourth Avenue Locals replaced Brighton trains on Queens Boulevard, and new R27-30 cars with the RR route designation eventually replaced the old Standards. Six years later when the Chrystie Street connection opened, a new EE service provided the Broadway–Queens Boulevard service, operating only between Whitehall Street in Lower Manhattan and Forest Hills. Ironically, IND R1-9 equipment was assigned initially to this route, replacing the newer R27-30 cars, marking only the third time that R1-9 equipment operated on the Broadway BMT line.

In 1976 the EE was eliminated in favor of an extended N (Sea Beach Line) route from Manhattan. Since 1987, Fourth Avenue Local trains have returned to Queens Boulevard, rechristened as R trains, and continue to provide this service 24/7.

The final construction project in this troika of IND-BMT linkages was completed in 1956, but it has the longest and most unusual history of the three. The project, known as the Grant Avenue ramp, consisted of a short ramp that linked the IND A train's Euclid Avenue terminal station, on the Brooklyn-Queens border, with the BMT's Fulton Street elevated line two stations away at 80th Street and Liberty Avenue. A new intermediate underground station at Grant Avenue was also built. But first some history is needed.

The Fulton Street Elevated originally opened in 1889 and stretched the length of Brooklyn, from the East River waterfront to Grant Avenue, then known as City Line in deference to Brooklyn's status as a separate city before 1898. That year the Fulton el was extended to Park Row in Lower Manhattan via the Brooklyn Bridge, and by 1915 a new Dual Contracts extension carried it beyond City Line to Lefferts Avenue in Richmond Hill, Queens. The extension was built to permit heavy steel subway cars to use its tracks; the original structure could not accommodate steel cars and thus forced the Fulton el service to rely on obsolete wooden cars.

As noted in the first chapter, the 1940 unification saw the immediate razing of the Fulton Street Elevated between Brooklyn Bridge and Rockaway Avenue in Ocean Hill, as the new A train subway below Fulton Street, opened in 1936, rendered the old el redundant. This route was unusual because for virtually its entire length in Brooklyn it was built directly below an old elevated line with the obvious intent of replacing the overhead trains, along both Fulton Street and Pitkin Avenue. Even though part of the BMT el was rebuilt to carry steel cars, much of it never received any upgrade, making it one of the first elevated lines razed after the 1940 unification.

However, the Fulton el did not completely vanish right away. Since the initial A line subway route ended at Rockaway Avenue, beyond there the el remained for another sixteen years, connected to the A train via a free transfer, but its days were numbered because it could not accommodate steel cars. The truncated el also accommodated a second service (14th Street–Fulton Street) which operated between Eighth Avenue/14th Street and Lefferts Boulevard using the Canarsie Line and the Fulton el via a connection

It's June 1955, and platform extension work is under way at the 104th Street–Oxford Avenue Station on the Fulton Street el above Liberty Avenue in Ozone Park. This stretch of elevated was retained; A trains still use it today. The three-story brick buildings on the left are characteristic of housing on both sides of the Brooklyn-Queens border. NYTM

It's October 1955, and platform extension work is being done at Lefferts Blvd., the terminal of the Fulton el and soon the A train. The intersection was a busy commercial crossroads for the Richmond Hill neighborhood. NYTM

Mayor Wagner greets the first motormen to pilot an IND train to Rockaway, in June 1956. NYTM

The Far Rockaway/Mott Avenue subway station is opened for business in January 1958, completing the Rockaway subway extension project. The radio station WNYC covered the event. NYTM

at the Atlantic Avenue Station. Long term, the plan for the A train subway to replace the el completely did happen, but it was also tied into a larger scheme to run subway trains to the Rockaway peninsula in Queens.

World War II's end allowed the A train gradually to march east and replace the Fulton el completely. In December 1946 it went one station further to Broadway Junction, and in November 1948 an additional four-station extension carried A trains to Euclid and Pitkin Avenues, near the Queens border. A new subway yard just beyond Euclid was also opened as well. For the next eight years Brooklyn's Pitkin Avenue hosted both the IND underground and the BMT aboveground, but in 1956 this duplication ended when the Grant Avenue ramp was opened. A trains were operated through to Lefferts Boulevard on the elevated above Liberty Avenue, which because of its newer construc-

Subway Sun from June 1956 announcing the beginning of IND service to the Rockaways.
www.thejoekorner.com

tion could handle the steel subway cars. The remaining Fulton el route, primarily atop Pitkin Avenue, was razed. But the story doesn't end here.

In 1952 New York City bought the Long Island Rail Road's Rockaway Beach Line between Rego Park and the Rockaway Peninsula, encompassing an inverted letter "T" route that had branches to Far Rockaway and Rockaway Park. This line intersected the Fulton El structure at Liberty Avenue just east of its Rockaway Boulevard Station in Ozone Park, Queens. While the original idea was to link the old LIRR route with the Queens Boulevard subway near the latter's 63rd Drive Station, that idea was abandoned because of the extremely heavy travel already on the Queens Boulevard route and to save additional construction costs. Thus, the IND was extended to Rockaway on the old LIRR route using a connection between the two lines where they intersect. The LIRR continued to serve Far Rockaway via its still-active branch line through Nassau County to Valley Stream but severed itself from the line on the Rockaway Peninsula.

The entire project was put in service in a two-month period in the spring and early summer of 1956. On April 29, IND trains began operating all the way to Lefferts Boulevard. Sixty days later, on June 28, IND service crossed Jamaica Bay for the first time. As the Transit Authority's house organ *Transit* proclaimed, New York had another "subway that goes to the sea." The A train, in fact, is the only New York subway route that covers parts of three formerly separate rail operators in its thirty-five-mile run between Inwood (Manhattan) and Far Rockaway (Queens)—IND, BMT, and LIRR. If the A train were somehow continued east one station into Nassau County on today's still-active LIRR Far Rockaway Branch, the next station would be Inwood, an unincorporated community in the town of Hempstead.

So in the roughly two years between October 1954 and June 1956, NYCTA completed three major physical linkages between the IND and BMT lines that permitted more trains, fewer transfers, and more logical routings. Redundant elevated routes and their attendant maintenance costs were eliminated. Service was extended for over twelve miles to a series of neighborhoods that never had subway service until 1956.

The BMT-IND story was not over. In 1967, upon the completion of the Chrystie Street Connection and related construction in Brooklyn and Manhattan, the BMT and IND took their courtship to the ultimate level and entered into a full-scale marriage (see Chapter 19). And today, forty-seven years later, the BMT-IND marriage is still alive and well.

13

1955: Sunshine Returns to Third Avenue

The Third Avenue Elevated opened in 1878 in Manhattan, originally from South Ferry to 129th Street. By 1887 it had vaulted the Harlem River into the newly developing Annexed District, today known as the Bronx. In stages it was extended northward along North Third Avenue (today simply Third) to Tremont Avenue (1891), Fordham Road (1901), and Bronx Park (1902). By 1890 the Third Avenue El was owned by the Manhattan Railway Company, along with parallel routes on Second, Sixth, and Ninth Avenues. In 1903 the new Interborough Rapid Transit Company (IRT) leased, for 999 years, the entire Manhattan Railway network in Manhattan and the Bronx, because the IRT wanted to coordinate the el's operations with its new subway routes to avoid possibly ruinous competition.

The original Third Avenue El route was rebuilt with a third track and express stations in the 1913–1916 period as part of the Dual Contracts; this work also included a new extension from Fordham Road to Gun Hill Road in 1920. In 1923–24, 470 open-vestibule cars were rebuilt with closed vestibules and remote-controlled doors that could be operated by one conductor; these were known as MUDC (multiple unit door control) cars and ran on all of Manhattan's elevated routes.

While the elevateds are important to New York's history because they were the first real rapid transit in the city, the success of the subways and the advent of heavy motor traffic on city streets became arguments to eliminate elevated lines, particularly in Manhattan.

By the 1930s, there was widespread agitation to remove the older, nineteenth-century els in Manhattan and Brooklyn. The unsightliness of the structures, constant noise from passing trains, and lack of sunlight on the streets below were all cited as the principal causes of lowered real estate values on Midtown Manhattan avenues that were astride the el routes. The first removal occurred on December 4, 1938, when the Sixth Avenue El stopped running and was razed soon afterward. Under subway unification in June 1940, the Board of Transportation immediately closed and razed the IRT's Ninth Avenue and Second Avenue (north of 60th Street) routes as well as the Fulton Street and Fifth Avenue/Third Avenue routes in Brooklyn. By June 1942 the entire Second Avenue line was abandoned, leaving the Third Avenue El as the sole Manhattan overhead rail transit route.

Third Avenue El enters its last decade in 1945 in Lower Manhattan. Note the Rheingold beer ad on the right. NYTM

About 1950, on a gray wintry day, a southbound train is entering the 53rd Street Station. The Chrysler Building is in the middle distance. NYTM

With the end of World War II and the resumption of new commercial construction projects, political pressure was again raised to remove the Third Avenue Elevated. The structure was by now nearly seventy years old, and the old wooden cars were running on borrowed time. It was clear that if the line were to survive beyond the mid-1950s it would need a major rebuilding and new trains, both of which were beyond the means of a cash-strapped Board of Transportation that was trying to keep the fare at ten cents.

In 1951 the city's voters approved a $500 million bond issue to build a Second Avenue subway to provide the track capacity to replace the Third Avenue El, plus other capital projects. With that money supposedly in the bank, Third Avenue service was gradually reduced. In December 1950 trains stopped running between Chatham Square and South Ferry; in March 1952 service south of 149th Street was completely eliminated between 7:00 PM and 6:00 AM every weekday and continuously from Friday night

1948, looking southbound toward the 149th Street Station, in the Hub district of the Bronx. NYTM

A northbound train is entering the 59th Street Station in 1949. Third Avenue was a hub of small retail and eating establishments at most el stations. NYTM

129th Street and Third Avenue in 1952, showing the old terminal that was used for short-turn local trains. A train of ex-BMT Q types is traveling southbound from the Bronx to Manhattan on a downtown express. The station's Victorian architecture stands out. NYTM

Looking uptown as a southbound express train charges through 34th Street Station, 1952. The station overpass is a remnant of the days when el shuttles connected this station to the old Long Island Rail Road ferry slip at the East River. The ferries stopped in 1925; the el shuttle followed in 1930. NYTM

through Monday morning. In December 1953 the City Hall branch was closed, making Chatham Square the south terminal. This final terminal, far removed from the downtown business district, was used weekdays only and lasted barely a year and a half. The el south of 149th Street was completely closed on May 12, 1955. While Third Avenue trains would continue to operate between 149th Street and Gun Hill Road, all passengers traveling to or from Manhattan would now have to transfer to the IRT Lexington or Seventh Avenue subways at 149th Street.

While the el's future was being debated, different interest groups lined up for and against retaining the line. On the pro-demolition side were the NYCTA and the city government. The TA would rid itself of the el's operating and maintenance costs, rather high figures considering the age of the structure and its obsolete technology, such as small coal stoves in the station waiting rooms to provide winter heat. The city was gambling that the el's removal would lead to much new real estate development along its

In March 1955, the Transport Workers Union Local 100 sponsored a series of demonstrations to save the el. This one is at 149th Street Station, in the background along with a Surface Transportation bus whose driver, also a TWU member, is no doubt sympathetic. TWU Local 100 archives

Another demonstration to save the el, this time in Manhattan. TWU officials Michael Quill and Matthew Guinan are in front flanking the person on stilts. A sign about halfway up the group suggests that the el should not be razed until the Second Avenue subway is built. TWU Local 100 archives

The TWU "save the el" movement is now on 116th Street. The Cosmo Theatre, just west of Third Avenue, is showing two movies that are still remembered today. TWU Local 100 archives

96th Street and Third Avenue: demolition continues as a Surface Transportation bus goes northbound on the M101 route toward Fort George. NYTM

Looking south at 125th Street and Third Avenue as the el is dismantled early in 1956. Two Surface Transportation buses are shown here, a major transfer point on its route network. NYTM

In 1956, old Third Avenue El cars were stored on the Dyre Avenue Line near East 180th Street prior to scrapping. NYTM

route and a resultant increase in property tax revenue. For the stretch between 14th and 86th Streets this proved to be the case soon after the el was gone; below 14th and above 96th Streets did not appreciably increase in value or attractiveness until the very late twentieth century. Real estate developers were also, naturally, glad to see the el go. The operators of bus routes on Third Avenue (Surface Transportation Corporation), Second Avenue (NYCTA), and Lexington Avenue (NYC Omnibus Corporation) all foresaw an increase in bus riders and resultant fare revenues.

On the anti-demolition side were the line's remaining regular users, the many small neighborhood businesses that relied on the el for customers, and the Transport Workers Union. While the approximately six hundred el workers were reassigned to other positions and none lost their jobs, the TWU still felt that long term these six hundred positions would be lost to attrition.

149th Street–Third Avenue subway station, where el customers riding the remaining portion of the line to the north now must transfer to the subway in order to continue into Manhattan. TWU Local 100 archives

Escalators that connected the subway and elevated stations at 149th Street (the Bronx Hub). This was a key transfer point for many years, until the el north of 149th Street was closed in 1973. TWU Local 100 archives

Introduction of new IRT rolling stock on the Lexington and Seventh Avenue lines, beginning with the R17 cars in October 1955, permitted faster operation and additional scheduled trains and was cited as another justification for closing the Third Avenue el. The passage of the Second Avenue subway bond issue was another argument for demolition. The bottom line was both the city government and larger, influential business interests wanted the seventy-seven-year old el removed.

And so it was on Thursday evening, May 12, 1955, that the last el train departed Chatham Square at 6:04 PM and arrived about an hour later at Gun Hill Road. Manhattan's last elevated line was now history.

North of 149th Street, the Third Avenue el's Bronx stub continued running for another eighteen years, until it was closed on April 29, 1973. It functioned as a local train between connections with the IRT subways at Gun Hill Road on the north and 149th Street on the south; transfers were available at both stations. Population losses in the south-central Bronx were the stated reason for the 1973 closing. To replace the el, new bus service was created, stopping only at the el station locations, with free transfers to and from the subways at Gun Hill Road and 149th Street.

Nearly sixty years after the Third Avenue Elevated was razed in Manhattan, the Second Avenue subway is finally under construction, and the Lexington Avenue subway remains the most crowded trunk line on the entire system.

14

1956: Fifth Avenue Coach Becomes Number One

In 1954 the Chicago-based Omnibus Corporation, which owned Fifth Avenue Coach and New York City Omnibus, decided to concentrate on nontransit businesses and divest itself of its two remaining urban bus operations. The firm had already sold Chicago Motor Coach Company to the Chicago Transit Authority in 1952 for $16.5 million, and two years later local executives of Fifth Avenue and NYC Omnibus purchased the stock of the two companies from the Omnibus Corporation and adopted New York City Omnibus as the corporate name for the combined firm.

Even though the Fifth Avenue/NYC Omnibus operation was now under New York–based control, the transition was almost meaningless to the public. The more important change was that Fifth Avenue and NYC Omnibus were no longer distinctive operations. Since the unique Fifth Avenue Coach double-deck buses had been retired in 1953, both sets of buses were nearly identical-looking single-deck GMC vehicles, and fares on both became a straight fifteen cents after 1956. Fifth Avenue's no-standee policy, two-man operation, and higher fares were all memories.

In 1956 the owners of the combined New York operations rechristened it Fifth Avenue Coach Lines, Incorporated. The original Fifth Avenue routes were now the FACO Division; the original NYC Omnibus routes were now the NYCO Division. The buses were painted green and cream (or tan) and lettered "Fifth Avenue Coach Lines" on the sides, but transfers were not honored between the two divisions. The bus routes, vehicle and garage assignments, and seniority lists did not change.

The same year Fifth Avenue's owners saw a new conquest on the horizon—Surface Transportation System, the successor to the Third Avenue Railway (see Chapter 4). Surface had been operating under bankruptcy court protection since June 1949. While it was still in that state in 1956, Fifth Avenue's management felt that the two companies would be better off together instead of competing. Accordingly, on December 17, 1956, Fifth Avenue's management purchased Surface outright because it believed that the two companies with pooled equipment and access to Fifth Avenue's more modern repair facilities, could be profitable.

Upon the takeover, Fifth Avenue created an operating subsidiary named Surface Transit Inc. for the new acquisition. The combined Fifth Avenue Coach–Surface network now controlled the vast majority of Manhattan's bus routes (exceptions were two

Beginning in 1948, Surface Transportation purchased large numbers of Mack buses to replace both its remaining streetcars and to replace pre–World War II buses. This one is #1914 on route BX1 southbound on the Grand Concourse at Fordham Road, in 1952. The fare is ten cents. The Dollar Savings Bank tower in the background was a familiar landmark to generations of Bronx residents. Motor Bus Society

NYCO #386 is a Yellow 740 rebuild and is working the 14th Street crosstown route about 1955, about to cross Third Avenue heading west. There are three transit modes visible in this photo: the bus, the Third Avenue El in its last days, and the entrance to the 14th Street–Canarsie BMT subway's Third Avenue Station. Motor Bus Society

NYC Omnibus #3003, a GMC TDH 4509, shown on the 79th Street crosstown route in the early 1950s. Motor Bus Society

Publicity photo of Fifth Avenue Coach GMC #2619, new in 1958. Riverside Church is in the background. Motor Bus Society

Avenue B and East Broadway Transit Company routes and five New York City Transit Authority routes), all Bronx routes, and a significant operation in the southern half of Westchester County. Fifth Avenue Coach was now the largest urban bus company in North America, and its biggest routes were located where high population density and relatively light private car competition combined to create a good market for urban bus service.

As was the case with the FACO/NYCO division breakdown, even though Surface Transit Inc. was legally a Fifth Avenue Coach subsidiary, to the average customer it was still a totally separate bus company. Garages, routes, union agreements, and seniority lists remained unchanged; transfers were not honored between the two companies. Its

Publicity photo of the interior of a FACO GMC bus similar to #2619, showing the wraparound rear seating arrangement adapted at that time. Motor Bus Society

It's the summer of 1959, and pictured here is a varied collection of Mack and GMC buses, clearly showing the amalgamation of Fifth Avenue Coach and Surface Transit. The buses are waiting for the crowds heading home from Orchard Beach. Motor Bus Society

Surface Transportation Mack bus #2998 is on route M104/Broadway, operating northbound at 79th Street in May 1957. An entrance to the uptown IRT subway is at right. Surveyor's signs on the street indicate the beginning of construction to lengthen the subway platform. NYTM

buses were relettered "Surface Transit Inc." but did not display the words "Fifth Avenue Coach." One result was that Surface drivers continued to earn a few cents per hour less than Fifth Avenue's comparable workers—in 1961, for example, Surface drivers earned $2.495 per hour while Fifth Avenue men earned $2.57. Another difference was that Surface Transit buses were generally in poor condition compared to Fifth Avenue's.

The route structures, similarly, were not combined. For example, Surface Transit operated two important mid-Manhattan crosstown routes, on 42nd and 59th Streets; buses were dispatched from a garage at 126th Street and Second Avenue instead of from NYC Omnibus garages located closer to the routes—at 54th Street and Ninth Avenue or 100th Street and Lexington Avenue, for example. The first outward sign of the takeover occurred in 1957 and 1958 when some FACO and NYCO buses were transferred to

Surface garages to replace some of the oldest Surface Transit rolling stock. These buses were renumbered and relettered for Surface but otherwise retained their Fifth Avenue green and tan (or cream) paint schemes. Later on, some Surface buses were repainted in Fifth Avenue green and cream, and new ones delivered in 1959 and 1960 were in paint schemes identical to Fifth Avenue's buses. Others remained in their original Surface Transit red and ivory livery. The result was that on Surface routes passengers had a collage of bus colors, some new and shiny, others old and faded.

A sticky and unusual labor dispute occurred a few years later when New York City's Traffic Department was planning the conversion of Third and Lexington Avenues to one-way operation. Fifth Avenue's management had fought, without success, one-way conversions between 1948 and 1957 on Broadway, Sixth, Seventh, Eighth, Ninth–Columbus, and Tenth–Amsterdam Avenues. This time management saw little point in fighting. Originally announced for implementation in March 1959, the actual one-way conversion was planned to begin in July 1960.

The labor dispute stemmed from the planned operation of buses under the new traffic arrangement. Surface Transit operated route M101 along Third Avenue, the vestige of the last streetcar operation in midtown and downtown Manhattan; this route was nearly twelve miles long and covered territory from City Hall to 190th Street and Amsterdam Avenue, traversing (south to north) Park Row, Bowery, Third Avenue, 125th Street, and Amsterdam Avenue. Fifth Avenue Coach's NYCO division operated two routes along Lexington—the #3 was a straight shot between 23rd and 131st Streets; the #4 ran between 8th Street and Fourth Avenue and 146th Street and Lenox Avenue via Fourth Avenue, 24th Street, Lexington Avenue, 116th Street, and Lenox Avenue. Under the one-way operation Surface Transit's M101 would provide all of the service, and the #3 and #4 routes would be eliminated. The Fifth Avenue Coach #2/Madison Avenue route would be rerouted at 116th Street to a new north terminal at 146th Street and Lenox, in order to cover the former #4 route. Some drivers, mostly with low seniority, would be transferred from Fifth Avenue to Surface Transit assignments to provide the revised service, but no jobs were eliminated.

Fifth Avenue's management and the Transport Workers Union leadership both agreed on the new driver assignments in June 1960, prior to the beginning of the one-way operations. A dissident group of TWU members opposed this plan, citing loss of seniority rights and slightly lower base hourly pay. When this group failed to convince the union leadership to change the plan, the dissidents walked off the job for a few days in late June 1960, without TWU approval. Even TWU President Michael Quill, usually known for his verbal slings directed toward company managements, referred to the striking drivers as "birdbrains and crackpots."[1] The dispute was settled after five days

1. *New York Times* (June 29, 1960).

when it was agreed that the Fifth Avenue drivers and buses would provide the short-turn service (between 23rd and 125th Streets) along Third and Lexington Avenues. The buses would be lettered for Surface Transit and bore the same M101 route number as the full route.

Once the intraunion labor issue was settled, the combined Fifth Avenue–Surface operation continued to operate successfully until early 1962. Early that year, an aggressive new management group gained stockholder control. Six weeks afterward, Fifth Avenue Coach, Surface Transit, and their distinctive buses were only a memory. This story will be covered in Chapter 16.

15

1957–1959: IRT West Side Improvement

In 1957, NYCTA began a major rehabilitation of the IRT's Broadway–Seventh Avenue Line between Times Square and 96th Street. Dubbed the West Side IRT Improvement Project, it was the agency's first complete rehabilitation of a major route segment. The route had not substantially changed its operating patterns since its 1904 opening, despite the increasing demands placed on it over the years as Upper Manhattan and the Bronx greatly increased in population and resultant subway riders. The three keys to modernizing the line were (1) reworking service patterns at 96th Street, where the branch serving Lenox Avenue and East Bronx routes diverged from the branch serving upper Broadway and the northwestern Bronx; (2) rebuilding the 96th Street station by adding new south access at 94th Street and closing the 91st Street Station; and (3) lengthening station platforms at 50th, 59th, 66th, 79th, and 86th Streets to 525 feet to accommodate ten-car trains.

Historically, four separate services were operated between 96th and Chambers Streets. Originating from the Lenox Avenue branch were two full time services—the Seventh Avenue Local between 145th Street/Lenox Avenue and South Ferry and the Seventh Avenue Express between East 180th Street or Dyre Avenue and Flatbush Avenue, Brooklyn.[1] Originating from the upper Broadway branch were two more services—the Broadway–Seventh Avenue Local between 137th Street and South Ferry (weekdays only) and the full-time Broadway–Seventh Avenue Express between 242nd Street/Van Cortlandt Park and New Lots Avenue, Brooklyn.

The key constraint and biggest construction phase involved station platforms. North of 96th Street (103rd through 242nd Streets) the platforms had been lengthened to ten cars in 1948, but because such work had not been performed at the six stations from 50th to 91st Streets (50th, 59th, 66th, 79th, 86th, and 91st Streets), any train making those stops was restricted to a five- or six-car consist. As a result, 96th Street and Broadway was a major choke point. The Seventh Avenue Local and the Broadway–Seventh Avenue Ex-

---

1. Before August 1952 the north terminal for Seventh Avenue Express trains was at 180th Street–Bronx Park Station, a short one-station stub that extended north of the East Tremont Avenue–West Farms Square Station. After that it was razed, and Seventh Avenue trains terminated at East 180th Street.

press had to cross between two tracks in order to make their correct stops south of 96th Street. The crossover moves delayed trains and slowed service. The short local trains also caused delays and crowding at express stops when express riders transferring to locals had to run along part of the platform to catch their train. The rolling stock on the locals, typically classic IRT cars of World War I vintage, also needed replacement.

NYCTA created a multitasked (to borrow a current expression) approach to improving service.

- The 96th Street crossover moves would be eliminated by creating two straight-line services. All trains to/from 242nd Street/Van Cortlandt Park (today's #1 train and the short-lived #9 train) were routed on the local tracks south of 96th Street (including short turns to/from Dyckman and 137th Streets). Trains to/from Dyre Avenue/East 180th Street or 145th Street and Lenox Avenue (today's #2 and #3 trains respectively) were routed on the express tracks south of 96th Street.
- Ninety-Sixth Street Station would be rebuilt and extended southward, where a new 94th Street mezzanine, fare controls, and street staircases would be constructed on both sides of Broadway between 93rd and 94th Streets. The side local train platforms, unique to 96th Street, would hereafter only be used for access between the north end street stairs and the express platforms via an underpass at that location. The new 94th Street access had a mezzanine between the platforms and the street. The 91st Street local stop would close once the rebuilt 96th Street Station opened.
- Local stations at 50th, 59th/Columbus Circle, 66th, 79th, and 86th Streets would have their platforms extended to allow ten-car trains of new equipment (525 feet). Seventy-Second Street Station's express platforms would also be modified to allow ten-car local trains to stop there. Fluorescent lighting would be installed as well.
- A New "Hi-Speed Local" service would operate on the Upper Broadway line between 242nd Street and South Ferry, replacing the two original services. New R22 cars, part of an order totaling 450 for the West Side IRT lines, would be assigned to this service, and signal replacements were made on the entire line. The result would be that the new local service between 242nd Street and 14th Street was scheduled for forty-one minutes, the same time as the old Broadway–Seventh Avenue Express service between those stops.[2]

The station platform extensions between 96th and 50th Streets were the most significant, visible, and disruptive of the entire project. Because the stations were built di-

2. As cited in the *New York Times* (January 26, 1959).

A survey photo of a street directly above a subway station slated for platform lengthening. This is the northwestern corner of 80th Street and Broadway in May 1957, directly above where the 79th Street Station would be lengthened as part of the IRT West Side Improvement. Note the Zabar's sign among the storefronts on the left; this famous gourmet food establishment now occupies almost the entire block shown in the photo. NYTM

The 72nd Street Station, facing the north end of the southbound platform, prior to platform lengthening construction in August 1957. NYTM

Street-level platform lengthening construction to the 72nd Street Station proceeds in October 1957. Note how vehicular traffic is restricted to the single right lane. NYTM

In October 1957, we are looking south along Broadway from 71st Street. Temporary wood decking covers the platform work; Surface Transit and Fifth Avenue Coach buses move along Broadway. NYTM

rectly below the street surface, the platform extensions required tearing up streets and sidewalks at each station. Besides interfering with vehicular and pedestrian traffic, utilities at each location required relocation or protection from construction equipment. Gas, electric, telephone, sewer, and water lines were all affected. Heavy machinery had to be shoehorned in narrow lanes above the work to allow vehicular traffic to pass. It was almost like the early 1900s all over again when the line was first built, the major and obvious difference being the preponderance of motor vehicles on the street that had to be accommodated and the greater numbers of telephone and electric conduits below ground.

Above the 86th Street Station, looking south on Broadway; northbound traffic is facing the camera. Platform construction is about to start, evidenced by the wood barrier along the left traffic lane and the surveyor's markers. The bus is a Surface Transit Mack C49 on the M104/Broadway route. The long awning on the right sidewalk is for the Tip Toe Inn, a restaurant that was a West Side landmark until its 1964 closing. The Fink bread truck on the left is another old New York firm that is now gone. NYTM

96th Street Station, southbound side, September 1957. A separate local platform was located along the wall, requiring local trains to open doors on both sides. This arrangement ended after the station was rebuilt, after which local trains opened their doors only on the express side. The local platform was used for the signal tower and for access between the street and the express platform until 2010. A TA police officer stands at the extreme right. NYTM

96th Street in December 1957, showing construction of one of two new platform extensions to the south end, requiring modifications to tracks and support beams. NYTM

Completed platform at south end of 96th Street, April 1959. NYTM

Station rebuilding at 96th Street was the most complicated part of the project. The station had an unusual layout in that passengers entered from either the southeastern or southwestern corners and proceeded one flight down to a five-car local sidewall platform. Once there they could either board a local train, pass through a local train to one of two island express platforms, or go downstairs and then up using a cross-passage that connected both local and both express platforms. The layout was awkward and unwieldy.

94th Street mezzanine at the south end of 96th Street, shown when new in April 1959. NYTM

103rd Street Station in May 1952, after the earlier platform lengthening on the West Side IRT was completed. NYTM

Subway Sun notice from February 1959, announcing the beginning of the new IRT West Side "Hi-Speed Local" service. www.thejoekorner.com

The solution was multifaceted. First step was to close the local platforms to trains, with local trains opening doors on the express platforms only. The local platforms were retained for access between the street stairs and the express platforms via the existing underpass. The second step was building a new south end mezzanine, above the platforms, with turnstiles and a token booth, including street staircases to both sides of Broadway between 93rd and 94th Streets. This work was very complicated as it involved modifying supporting beams and walls in a very constrained area just below the street surface. The 91st Street local stop was closed once the rebuilt 96th Street Station went into service; it was only two and one-half blocks from the new 94th Street access.

The station platforms north of 96th Street had been lengthened previously for ten-car trains, so at least this portion of the line could accommodate longer trains. The local station platforms between Rector and 28th Streets were built in 1917–1918 to accommodate eight-car trains (later these would be lengthened to ten cars). But without platform lengthening on the critical middle stretch between 50th and 96th Streets, it would not be possible to run eight- or ten-car trains on the #1 Broadway Local.

The work went on for two years, from February 1957 until February 1959. An article in the *New York Times* on April 19, 1957, noted the disruptions that were occurring then because of the platform construction, under the headline "Rehabilitation of the West Side Subway Puts the Squeeze on Surface Transportation."[3] Broadway had already been changed to one-way south traffic below Columbus Circle so that disruptions were somewhat mitigated, but according to the article, they were still significant. By May 1958 NYCTA announced that the traffic disruptions would end by February 1959 and that the entire project would be completed by June 1959. As things turned out, the new subway services and renovated stations debuted on February 6, 1959. The following day, the *Times* reported that Mayor Wagner praised the completed project and used the occasion to pledge that the fifteen-cent fare would be retained for the balance of 1959.

New York Times (April 19, 1957).

The success of the West Side IRT Improvement Project can be measured by the fact that in the twenty-first century service patterns on the #1, #2, and #3 trains are still basically the same as existed in February 1959. The #2 and #3 trains still operate be-

---

3. The *New York Times* writer did not realize it, but the headline is a pun. "Surface Transportation" not only generically referred to the thousands of motor vehicles that operated along Broadway every day but was also the name of the private bus company that operated the M104/Broadway route directly atop the subway construction.

tween the Bronx (#2) or Harlem (#3) and terminals in Brooklyn (either Flatbush or New Lots Avenues), using the Broadway express tracks. Local service is still routed to the Upper Broadway tracks north of 96th Street.

One new improvement was completed in 2010. As part of a second-generation rebuilding of the 96th Street Station, the north end access was completely rebuilt. The two pairs of street stairs on the south side of 96th Street were replaced with a new entrance in the Broadway median between 95th and 96th Streets, finally eliminating the cumbersome and dingy underpass needed to move between the street and the two station platforms.

New York Times (May 20, 1958).

16

1962: Fifth Avenue Coach Suddenly Disappears

After its marriage in December 1956, the combined Fifth Avenue Coach/Surface Transit operation trundled on through 1961, profitable enough to attract outside investment interest. One such entrepreneur, Harry Weinberg, headed a group that owned and operated bus systems in Dallas, Scranton, and Honolulu. In 1961 Weinberg's group began buying Fifth Avenue's outstanding stock, quickly amassing nearly 69,000 of the total 883,000 common shares. At a chaotic stockholders meeting in May 1961 the Weinberg stockholder faction did not gain control, but it did not give up its quest. In November 1961 the Weinberg faction publicly accused the incumbent management (led by President John Moreland) of courting the cooperation of the TWU and the New York City government as a means of retaining its control, at the expense of stockholders. As part of its claim, the Weinberg faction filed a suit in the New York State Supreme Court attempting to stop Fifth Avenue's current management team and allied directors from spending funds in a proxy fight to keep themselves in office.[1] The Weinberg faction's legal counsel was Roy M. Cohn, the well-known attorney who first became a public figure in 1954 from his association with the late Senator Joseph McCarthy.

In December Fifth Avenue's management filed a counterpetition against Cohn's action, charging the Weinberg group with using its suit to "utter privileged libel." Further, it was charged that the Weinberg group had no factual basis for its claim that Fifth Avenue's management was trying clandestinely to court the TWU and the city government.[2]

In the background of the stockholder suits, labor strife continued to roil. The TWU contract with all New York City private bus operators (in the Bronx, Manhattan, and Queens) expired on November 30, 1961. Mayor Wagner brokered a thirty-day extension to prevent a strike and keep the talks going. At the beginning of January 1962, settlements were reached with all private bus companies except for Fifth Avenue and Surface Transit. Accordingly, a four-day strike occurred, as the TWU's "No Contract—No Work" policy was implemented. Once that dispute was settled the buses rolled, but bigger events were on the horizon—only no one knew this at the time.

1. *New York Times* (November 30, 1961).
2. *New York Times* (December 12, 1961).

TWU members walking the picket line during the January 1–4, 1962, strike again FACO. TWU President Michael Quill (right) is holding the sign that says "No Contract No Work." TWU Local 100 archives

Fifth Avenue Coach (FACO) bus returning to its garage in the early hours of January 1, 1962, at the beginning of a four-day TWU strike against the company. TWU Local 100 archives

One of the settlement terms of the January 1962 strike was that New York City gave Fifth Avenue and Surface authority to stop issuing transfers, creating a double-fare situation for many riders. The city also increased the payments it made to Fifth Avenue and Surface for transporting schoolchildren who used bus passes. It was hoped that these two moves would put the books in the black.

Once the January strike was over the Weinberg faction increased its pressure to take complete control at Fifth Avenue Coach. At the same time, another outside investor and transit operator, O. Roy Chalk, announced his intent to buy Fifth Avenue stock in order to obtain control. Chalk (1907–1995) was a flamboyant entrepreneur who headed Transportation Corporation of America. This firm controlled Trans-Caribbean Airlines and D.C. Transit System, the public bus operator in Washington, D.C. He had made unsuccessful overtures in the past to purchase the entire New York City Transit Authority subway and bus system, and before that the San Francisco Municipal Railway.

The Chalk attempt to buy Fifth Avenue died quickly, but the Weinberg faction succeeded. At a contentious stockholder meeting held on February 14, 1962, it managed to gain enough proxy votes to gain control. Five members of Weinberg's group gained seats on Fifth Avenue's board of directors, and two days later it elected Weinberg the new company chairman. One of the new Weinberg directors was Roy M. Cohn.

Right away, the new management made it clear that changes would be needed, in part because the company was losing money from the elimination of transfers that was part of the January strike settlement. Weinberg already had a reputation as an anti-union cost cutter, and he demanded that New York City permit a twenty-cent fare (with the five-cent transfer fee restored). He also proposed laying off eight hundred persons from Fifth Avenue's work force and the elimination of unprofitable service at night and on Sundays. The layoff proposal naturally stirred up the TWU and its international president, Michael Quill. The TWU voted to authorize a strike on March 2 if the new management went through with its threat to lay off any workers. The city government, for its part, refused to allow a fare increase but offered to negotiate other issues with the new management, which refused to rescind its layoff threat.

New York Times (March 2, 1962).

On Thursday, March 1, 1962, a cold, clear day that was already newsworthy because of a fatal jetliner crash at Kennedy Airport (then called New York International Airport or, informally, Idlewild) and the astronaut John Glenn's ticker-tape parade on lower Broadway, Fifth Avenue laid off twenty-nine light-duty employees. These men were street fare collectors, doormen, and watchmen—all former veteran bus operators who because of illness, injury, or age could no longer drive. The TWU immediately

FACO bus returns to its garage at the beginning of TWU strike on March 1, 1962. TWU Local 100 archives

FACO employees on light duty who were fired on March 1, 1962, precipitating the strike that brought down the company. TWU Local 100 archives

Strikers picketing outside the Fifth Avenue Coach garage at Ninth Avenue and 54th Street. Note sign on right that says "Weinberg-Cohen Contract Violation." Cohen is misspelled; it refers to Roy Cohn, the FACO board member and attorney. TWU Local 100 archives

Strikers, including the young daughters of one worker, picketing in March 1962. TWU Local 100 archives

The TWU's slogan during the March 1962 strike. TWU Local 100 archives

TWU President Michael Quill appearing on television during the March 1962 strike, with an empty chair reserved for no-show FACO president Harry Weinberg. TWU Local 100 archives

called a strike at the height of the evening rush hour. The *New York Times* on March 2 showed two photos on its front page—one showed Fifth Avenue packed with buses at 5:00 PM; the second one showed an avenue empty of buses twenty minutes later.

Within days it became clear that the Weinberg management had committed the serious mistake of waging simultaneous war with the TWU and the city government. The public was treated to the rare spectacle of Michael Quill and Mayor Robert Wagner on the same side of the table in public. Wagner publicly lambasted Weinberg and said that he would never operate a bus company in New York City. The city moved to have Fifth Avenue's and Surface's buses and garages seized by condemnation; the New York

West Farms Square in the Bronx during the strike, empty of its normal large contingent of Surface Transit buses. The bus on the left is a NYC Transit vehicle on the Q44 route, not affected by the strike. Note the trolley tracks in the middle, unused since 1948 but still embedded in the pavement. In the background is the 1904 elevated line on Boston Road; it still carries the #2 and #5 trains today. TWU Local 100 archives

Bus leaving its garage on March 23, 1962, after the strike ended with New York City seizing the buses and garages. The bus is now officially a MABSTOA vehicle despite the FACO lettering on the side, which will disappear quickly. TWU Local 100 archives

Picketing continued during the week of March 26, 1962, when Fifth Avenue Coach management announced it would attempt to operate, using newly hired nonunion workers, its original routes along Fifth Avenue, which did not resume operation right away. TWU members massed outside FACO headquarters on West 132nd Street and quickly brought an end to that ill-fated idea. Two days later MABSTOA resumed operation of the original Fifth Avenue routes as well. TWU Local 100 archives

State legislature quickly passed laws allowing this to occur, which Governor Nelson Rockefeller signed immediately. With the exceptions of the circa-1900 franchises issued for Fifth Avenue's original routes, those for the Omnibus Division and Surface Transit routes were found to be revocable extensions of franchises that had expired.

Accordingly, the state legislation created a Manhattan and Bronx Surface Transit Operating Authority (MABSTOA), a subsidiary agency of the New York City Transit Authority, to operate Fifth Avenue's entire route system. Part of the New York State law citation that created MABSTOA appears in this chapter; the new agency was created by amending the same Public Authorities law that had created the NYCTA nine years earlier. By March 22, New York City had seized, by legal condemnation, FACO's garages and buses in the Bronx, Manhattan, and Queens.

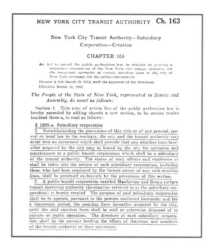

New York State Public Authorities Law March 1962
amendments that created MABSTOA.

Friday, March 23, 1962, saw the resumption of some service; the following day all routes operated, with the exception of the original Fifth Avenue routes on the namesake avenue.

New York Times (March 23, 1962).

By the end of March, with the exception of two routes, all of the former Fifth Avenue, New York City Omnibus, and Surface Transit lines were operating normally, charging a fifteen-cent fare but still not offering transfers.

In New York's long and often fractious transit history, nothing like this had ever occurred before or since. Public sector takeovers of private transit concerns were normally long, drawn-out affairs, ranging from the 1940 subway unification to the MTA's 2005–2006 takeover of the remaining private bus companies in New York City. The MABSTOA creation was accomplished, amazingly, in under two weeks.

A new FACO GM "fishbowl," model TDH 5301, is shown new in 1960. Also painted in bright yellow and green, this was one of ten buses equipped with factory air conditioning in a total order of 120. This bus was also repainted and renumbered after the MABSTOA takeover and lasted until about 1973.
Motor Bus Society

#1752, a 1948 Mack C-45 inherited from Surface Transit, is shown in May 1962 right after the MABSTOA takeover. The generally poor condition of Surface's equipment is obvious. This bus would be scrapped by 1963. NYTM

#2421 is a 1950 GMC TDH-4509, inherited from Fifth Avenue Coach, shown around 1963 after being repainted into NYCTA two-tone green. It was part of a large group of GMC buses that lasted on MABSTOA routes until 1967 and shows the much better condition of FACO's buses versus Surface Transit. NYTM

The reasons are simple. The new Fifth Avenue management team, in a six-week period, destroyed the largest privately operated urban bus system in the United States because it simultaneously antagonized the TWU unions and the city government. Weinberg's team created two enemies at once. No business can survive such an environment. The previous Fifth Avenue Coach management would never have allowed a comparable situation to develop. The situation was also helped because all of the important politicians, regardless of party affiliation, rightly saw the Fifth Avenue Coach issue as a major disruption to life, so Mayor Wagner, a Democrat, and Governor Rockefeller, a Republican, worked with the Republican leaders in the New York State legislature quickly to pass the amendments to the Public Authorities Law that created MABSTOA.

Fifth Avenue's management did continue to operate its Westchester County routes under the corporate moniker Westchester Street Transportation Company because that operation was not part of the MABSTOA takeover, so it remained in private hands. However, the Fifth Avenue Coach imprint evaporated quickly from the city of its birth. Its seized buses were quickly repainted in the Transit Authority's two-tone green paint scheme, and the famous slogan "Go the Motor Coach Way" disappeared overnight.

Today, over half a century later, MABSTOA still exists on paper, although from the public perspective all Manhattan and Bronx local bus operations are part of the New York City Transit Authority system and have full transfer privileges between all routes. Even more amazing is that MABSTOA's routes, including many identifying numbers, are still basically the same as in 1962, a major exception being the combined routes on Fifth and Madison Avenues resulting from the 1966 conversion of those thoroughfares to one-way traffic.

Fifth Avenue Coach remained alive as a corporate entity until 1973, though not necessarily a healthy one. During the 1962 strike a number of Fifth Avenue and Surface buses were taken to Westchester and remained in service there into the early 1970s.

The Weinberg management team that took Fifth Avenue to its sudden end in 1962 broke up a year later. Harry Weinberg was removed as president, replaced by the 1962 vice president, Lawrence Weissman. Weinberg himself moved to Hawaii in 1968, where he died, a very wealthy man, in 1990. The best-known member of the original Weinberg team was Roy Cohn, the flamboyant lawyer who severed his connections with Fifth Avenue in 1964 but who continued in the public eye right up until his 1986 death.

Fifth Avenue's bus operating days finally ended in 1969 when its owners sold the Westchester operations to Liberty Coaches. After 1962 Fifth Avenue also continued business as an investment company, but because it failed to follow U.S. Securities and Exchange Commission registration practices, it was fined, registered with the SEC, and went into receivership. After long and protracted court battles Fifth Avenue received two condemnation awards from New York City (in 1967 and 1970) that totaled $54 million. Emerging from receivership in 1971 with its cash windfall, it changed its name to South Bay Corporation, which in turn became privately held in 1973 and disappeared from the radar screen.

There is one final irony to the whole Fifth Avenue story. Liberty Coaches, which as noted bought Westchester Street Transportation in 1969, continues to be the contract operator for the entire Westchester County bus system. One route, created in 1980s, is an express service at a $7.50 fare along Central Avenue connecting White Plains, Scarsdale, and Tuckahoe with Mid-Manhattan, where the route follows Fifth Avenue southbound and Madison Avenue northbound. So today, fifty years later, Fifth Avenue's successor operator still runs buses on its old namesake avenues, and at a premium fare as well, just like Fifth Avenue's original owners might have intended.

17

1964: World's Fair, Blue Subways, Stainless Steel Subways

From the 1940 unification until 1964, the thousands of new subway cars purchased by the Board of Transportation and its successor, the New York City Transit Authority, with the exception of ten experimental 1948 cars, all had carbon steel car bodies that required periodic painting. In 1960, the Philadelphia Transportation Company (PTC) installed a fleet of 270 new stainless subway cars for its Market–Frankford subway-elevated route. Making the purchase even more attractive, the prime contractor and car fabricator, the Budd Company, built the new rolling stock at its manufacturing plant right in the Quaker City. The cars were an immediate success. Lighter that conventional carbon steel, the weight reduction translated into reduced electric power consumption. Stainless steel requires no painting, further reducing operating and labor costs.

Despite the advantages of stainless steel, in early 1963 NYCTA ordered 430 conventional new cars (parts of the R33 and R36 contracts) for the IRT #7 route in preparation for crowds traveling to the New York World's Fair at Flushing Meadow Park, which was scheduled to run from April through October in both 1964 and 1965. St. Louis Car Company was the contractor for this car order, worth nearly $48 million. While the cars retained carbon steel bodies, they were painted an attractive light blue and white livery and featured larger window panes than their predecessor vehicles. The cars were delivered between August 1963 and June 1964 and became World's Fair icons in their own right.

The World's Fair itself, which opened April 22, 1964, was expected to attract 70 million visitors in its two-season run—40 million in 1964 and 30 million in 1965. As things turned out, 51.6 million visitors were counted during its two six month runs—27.1 million in 1964 and 24.5 million.[1] That number, while certainly substantial, was a disappointment to the fair's management and a financial bath to its investors, who generally recouped about half of what they paid for the fair corporation's bonds. However, millions of fair visitors arrived on the #7 subway and on the Long Island Rail Road's Port Washington Branch, which in 1964 was not a corporate cousin of the subways. Reflecting the automobile-centric society of the 1960s, the General Motors (29 million visitors), Chrysler Corporation (18.8 million), and Ford Motor (14.9 million) pavilions

1. *New York Times* (October 19, 1965): 45.

1964–1965 World's Fair, looking at the Unisphere, its official symbol. The Swiss Sky Ride crosses the fair site in the foreground. Queens Museum

Common entrance for LIRR and subway riders arriving at the 1964–1965 World's Fair, shown on a busy day. Queens Museum

Broadside view of R33-36 IRT World's Fair cars, when new. NYTM

R33-36 World's Fair cars at Willets Point Station. NYTM

ranked first, fourth, and sixth as individual fair attractions over the two-season run.[2] The LIRR had a small exhibit, but the New York City Transit Authority did not showcase itself beyond the new R33-36 rolling stock.

A byproduct of the World's Fair was Shea Stadium, the New York Mets's new home park, which opened five days before the fair itself and remained in use for forty-five seasons. Its replacement, Citi Field, is next door to its predecessor. The R33-36 rolling stock no doubt carried a large percentage of the nearly 95 million fans who attended Mets games at Shea Stadium from 1964 through 2008.[3] Since the Mets remain firmly

2. Ibid.

3. According to www.baseball-reference.com, the Mets drew a total of 94,775,000 customers to Shea Stadium in its forty-five-season history (1964–2008).

New York Times (June 26, 1963) article announcing that NYC Transit Authority
had awarded the Budd Company the R32 contract.

planted in Queens in their new stadium, the #7 will continue that line's baseball tradition for years to come.

The R33-36 car fleet would eventually be overhauled in the mid-1980s. The cars were retrofitted with air conditioning[4] and repainted, along with the R26-28-29 IRT fleet, in a deep red exterior livery that earned then the "Redbird" moniker. The last cars in the R36 fleet ran until November 3, 2003, appropriately still on the #7 route. They were considered the best IRT cars ever built in the 1947–1964 era.

The Budd Company did not give up trying to get a significant car order from New York. In 1948 Budd had built an experimental ten-car train for New York, the R11. It was never mass produced, but Budd continued to look at New York as a potential customer and in June 1963 won the six-hundred-car order for the R32 car class, destined for the IND and BMT divisions. Soon its Red Lion Plant in northeastern Philadelphia was humming with the work of fabricating the new cars. At the time, it was the largest rail passenger car order ever in the United States.

The purchase was announced in the *New York Times* on June 26, 1963. TA Chairman Joseph O'Grady termed the R32 contract a "fabulous buy" because the TA would save an estimated six million dollars in operating and maintenance expenses over a projected thirty-five-year lifespan compared with conventional carbon steel cars.

Interestingly, one minor modification had to be done on the R32s prior to delivery. Because of their lighter weight, the first cars tested proved to have vertical clearances that were too high for safe tunnel operation. When the car body was mounted on its trucks (the pair of wheel and axle assemblies under each car), it did not rest far enough to provide the required two inches of clearance between the car roof and the tunnel

4. Except for the single unit R33 cars that operated on the #7 line, which were never equipped with air conditioning.

New York Times (September 10, 1964) article about the R32 cars operating on
the New York Central Railroad to Grand Central Terminal.

roof. To correct the problem, each car's body bolster was modified at a total cost of
about $21 per car.

Indeed the R32 was a fabulous buy. The new fleet was introduced in an unusual ceremony on September 9, 1964, when a factory-fresh eight-car train was operated on the
then–New York Central Railroad (now Metro-North) from Mott Haven Yard in the
Bronx to Grand Central Terminal. The idea was to showcase the new car fleet at Grand
Central and demonstrate that they could also operate on commuter rail tracks. To
make this move, the R32's third rail contact shoes had to be repositioned in order to use
New York Central's underrunning third rail system.

By 1966 all six hundred R32 cars were in service, primarily on the BMT Division's
Brighton, Sea Beach, and West End lines. When the Chrystie Street Connection opened
November 26, 1967, R32s made their first forays into Upper Manhattan and the Bronx
when they appeared on the D train. That same day the BMT and IND divisions officially merged to form the B Division, a moniker still used today. Chapter 18 has more
details about the Chrystie Street project. In the ensuing years the fleet operated on all B
Division routes.

In 1988–1989 the cars received a midlife overhaul that saw air conditioning installed.
When the first group of R32s was ready for scrapping in 2008, the fleet still numbered
596 out of the original six hundred.

As of this writing, about 220 R32 cars are still on the active roster, nearly half a century
after going into service. And this is only after one midlife overhaul. The cars were so well
built that it is expected that R32s will continue in service until 2017, when the cars will be
an amazing fifty-three years old. No other subway car that ran in New York will have
been in revenue service for such a long time. Indeed, the MTA reported on its website in
September 2012 that $25 million will be spent to upgrade the R32's brake and propulsion
systems to ensure safe and reliable operation until the cars are finally scrapped:

Maintenance on our R32 cars will keep them on the rails until new R179 cars are delivered.

With their once-gleaming stainless-steel bodies dulled by age and their windows scarred by the negative attention of vandals, MTA New York City Transit's R32 subway cars are living out their final years of service until the arrival of their replacements. In order to make those last trips go more smoothly, however, the cars are "having a little work done."

The "Brightliners," as the Budd-built cars were dubbed upon their introduction into service back in 1964, were the first large fleet of stainless steel cars purchased by New York City Transit and the first corrosion resistant cars placed in service since the ten experimental cars purchased in 1949 by the New York City Board of Transportation.

Thanks to the combination of stainless steel construction, efficient design and the efforts of New York City Transit's subway car maintenance forces, the cars have held up admirably for nearly half a century, serving riders on nearly every lettered line route. Currently operating on the A and C lines, the cars have a distinctive ribbed sided appearance, rather than the smooth sides of more modern subway cars.

Today, the remaining 222 cars out of the original 600-car fleet are rotating through the Coney Island Overhaul Facility at a pace of four cars per week undergoing a limited-scope maintenance makeover intended to improve their performance and reliability until they are replaced by the fleet of 300 new R179 cars, due to begin arriving in 2014.

"The work currently being performed on these cars will help increase customer comfort and insure service reliability until their replacements arrive," said Carmen Bianco, Senior Vice President of the Department of Subways.

With a projected cost of nearly $25 million, the scope of work includes upgrades to several major car components and systems including: air brakes, auxiliary electric, car body, couplers, car body hoses, door systems, propulsion systems, some HVAC work and trucks. Work will also include structural enhancements and the replacement of vandalized windows.

Work is scheduled for substantial completion by the end of this year with air conditioning and structural improvements wrapped up by the beginning of next year's hot weather season.

Ironically, while every subway car built for New York since the R32 order has included a stainless steel exterior, Budd never built another subway car for NYCTA. It did build 1,246 M1 and M3 commuter cars for the Long Island Rail Road and Metro-North Railroad (and Metro-North's predecessor railroad Penn Central) but could not win the R38, R40, R42, R44, and R46 car orders (which all went to St. Louis Car Company except the R46, which was awarded to Pullman-Standard). Yet the R32 has outlasted the

R32 train set, when new, at Coney Island Yard. The door exteriors were originally royal blue. When the cars were rehabilitated in the late 1980s, replacement stainless steel doors were installed, without a painted finish. NYTM

Publicity photo of NYCTA bus with the Unisphere in the background. NYCTA operated two special routes between the Fair and Brooklyn. NYTM

R38, R40, and R44 cars and its Budd brethren M1 cars (LIRR and Metro-North), which were all newer. The R32 is testament to the Budd Company, which built quality railroad and rapid transit cars from the 1930s until the 1980s.

Thus, the 1964–1965 World's Fair is not only remembered for the event itself but for the two subway car fleets that entered service during those years and in some cases continue to run fifty years later.

18

1966: Mike Quill's Last Hurrah

After the New York City Transit Authority (NYCTA) was created in 1953, the Transport Workers Union (TWU) continued to represent the vast majority of New York's transit labor force. As noted in Chapter 10, the TWU got a huge boost in 1954 when it won a NYCTA-wide representation election in which it gained collective bargaining rights for all NYCTA workers except for Queens and Staten Island Bus Division workers, who remained with the Amalgamated Transit Union. The result was that labor relations under the NYCTA remained relatively peaceful for the next decade. Two labor disputes noted in earlier chapters of this book—in 1957 (subway motormen) and 1960 (Fifth Avenue Coach bus drivers)—involved dissident labor groups that were opposed to the TWU's leadership. Both disputes were quashed, resulting in continuing TWU hegemony over transit labor representation.

Every other December 31 beginning in 1955, NYCTA labor contracts expired at midnight. New York City residents were treated to continuing and nerve-tingling news reports of a threatened transit strike at dawn on New Year's Day of the new even-numbered year. The TWU postured, threatened to strike, and made outrageous-sounding public demands, such as a four-day, thirty-two-hour week for its members. Mike Quill was a master at using the media to the TWU's advantage. He would often say that "negotiations are hopelessly deadlocked" in his thick Irish brogue. The negotiators for the city and the Transit Authority would be quoted as saying that the TWU's demands could not be met without a fare increase, political poison to any incumbent mayor.

Behind the scenes, however, both sides would negotiate in private and somehow manage to hammer out a deal in the wee hours of January 1, so that the trains and buses continued to roll without interruption. The city government would often find some kind of payment to the NYCTA to prevent fares from increasing, such as one year when subsidies for reduced-fare student passes were funded from sources outside of the NYCTA's operating budget. Another year the city agreed to pay the cost of the Transit Authority police force (then separate from the New York City Police Department). Everyone would emerge looking good—the unions, the NYCTA management, and the mayor. It made for good newspaper copy and never-ending radio and television news reports. The results also cemented Mayor Robert Wagner's reputation as a friend of labor.

As 1965 droned to a close, two new events radically affected the biennial TWU-NYCTA labor negotiations. The first was the TWU leadership, specifically Mike Quill. He was in poor health due to a heart condition and concerned about his legacy, privately aware that he was unlikely to live much longer. His union members were growing increasingly restive as inflation reduced the value of their previous contract gains. The union's faces were also changing; by this time one-third of its members were black or Hispanic. The traditional Irish-dominated workforce that rallied behind Quill was beginning to retire, although its leadership remained Irish for many years afterward. Crime in the subways was now a big issue, and beginning in April 1965 police officers were assigned to ride every train between 8 PM and 4 AM. A general transit strike had never occurred in the history of the subway and bus systems. Quill knew that if he ever led such a strike, it would be January 1, 1966, or never again under his leadership. A strike would discipline the various intraunion factions into creating a unified public posture. It would also cement Quill's legacy as a pioneering labor leader.

The second event was a change in the city's leadership. In November 1965 New Yorkers elected a new mayor, John V. Lindsay, who replaced Robert Wagner after the latter's decision not to run for a fourth term. To Quill, Lindsay represented everything that he opposed, going back to his days as a young man in Ireland. Lindsay was an Anglo-Saxon Protestant, a resident of Manhattan's Upper East Side, a Yale University alumnus (undergraduate and law school), and a Republican. Quill was an Irish Catholic who had lived in the Bronx for many years, never completed his formal education beyond the age of twelve, and had been a Communist Party sympathizer in the 1930s and 1940s. As the columnist Jimmy Breslin succinctly commented, "Mike Quill looked at John Lindsay and saw the Church of England."[1]

Quill decided not to coexist peaceably with the new mayor. He saw Lindsay as a new and inviting target, and the media ate it up. The union leader was quoted as saying that "this man [Lindsay] knows nothing about working people" and "we don't like him." Quill also began referring to the new mayor as "Mayor Lindsley," continuing to display his (Quill's) media mastery. Clueless about the customary means to conduct transit labor negotiations, Lindsay finally joined the negotiations in late December, a week prior to his inauguration.

Earlier that month, a mediation panel was finally named to assist with the negotiations. This issue itself had dragged on since Lindsay's election, as the new mayor was reluctant to include Theodore Kheel to the panel. Kheel was the well-respected lawyer and veteran labor mediator who had been New York's transit labor guru since 1949. Lindsay associated Kheel with the Wagner administration's deal making, which he dis-

1. Vincent Cannato, *The Ungovernable City* (New York: Basic Books, 2001), 82; L. H. Whittemore, *The Man Who Ran the Subways: The Story of Mike Quill* (New York: Holt, Rinehart and Winston, 1968), 265.

liked. Under Mayor Wagner, Kheel was part of a three-man Transit Labor Board, which also included George Taylor and David Cole. Lindsay suggested ten new names from which to create a new panel, but in late November the TWU rejected all of them because Kheel was not included. Finally a compromise three-man panel was named in mid-December, which included Kheel, Nathan Feinsinger (the chairman), and Sylvester Garrett. While Feinsinger and Garrett were not from New York, Kheel respected them because they had long experience as arbiters for labor issues involving large corporations. Garrett was the permanent arbiter for United States Steel and the United Steelworkers Union; Feinsinger performed the same task for General Motors and the United Auto Workers.

The TWU's initial proposal was for a 30 percent wage increase, six weeks' vacation, a four-day week, pension improvements, and other assorted changes that according to Transit Authority estimates would add $300 million to its operating budget. While experienced negotiators knew that these proposals were opening salvos, Lindsay lectured Quill about "civic responsibility." The union chief reiterated that he was looking for a fair settlement for his membership, nothing more, and that all of the issues were on the table and negotiable. The TWU's key and real contract demand was to raise the hourly rates for skilled workers, such as subway motormen, to $4.00 per hour. The estimated cost for this increase above the existing contract was about $60 million. When the Transit Authority's initial settlement offer was in the neighborhood of $25 million, Quill dismissed it by saying "we won't take *bubkes* from a schmuck like you," signaling a clear rejection of the offer and an intentional insult to Lindsay. Quill's use of two Yiddish words, spoken in his Irish lilt, was a bow to his Jewish wife, herself a labor movement veteran and formerly secretary to Quill for many years.[2] The remark was continued proof of his mastery of the media.

The reality was that Quill now had the needed ammunition to call a general transit strike, which had never happened in New York's history up to this point. But the die was cast. So as January 1, 1966, dawned, two major events occurred simultaneously. John Lindsay became the city's 103rd mayor, and TWU's members struck the NYCTA system and most private bus carriers, shutting down all mass transit in the five boroughs with the single exception of Green Bus Lines in Queens, whose workers were Amalgamated Transit Union members. As the strike's first day was the Saturday of New Year's weekend, its effects were not really felt until Monday, January 3.

The strike's dozen days were full of events that became the stuff of legends. It was pure New York drama, featuring a dying Irish union boss and his Jewish wife, a new WASP mayor, and a veteran Jewish labor mediator attempting to settle the strike. Because New York State law forbade public employee strikes (the Condon-Wadlin Act)

2. Whittemore, *The Man Who Ran the Subways*, 279.

TWU pickets, January 1966, at Lenox Avenue and 145th Street in Harlem, above the IRT #3 train station. Old Yankee Stadium is in the background. TWU Local 100 archives

Pickets at Crosstown Bus Depot in Brooklyn. TWU Local 100 archives

Pickets at 207th Street and Broadway in Upper Manhattan, atop the IND A train terminus. TWU Local 100 archives

Railroad commuters, some of whom are displaced subway riders using the Long Island Rail Road, arriving at Penn Station in the early morning gloom of a rainy day during the 1966 strike. Penn Station was being demolished then, to be replaced by Madison Square Garden. TWU Local 100 archives

after the fourth day, Tuesday, January 4, Quill and the TWU were held in contempt of court for ignoring an order to go back to work. Quill was sent to jail and famously said, "The judge can drop dead in his black robes and we would not call off the strike." After a day in jail Quill suffered a heart attack and was rushed to Bellevue Hospital, while his union's vice presidents continued the negotiations. It then became public knowledge that he was not in good health, although no one knew at the time that he was indeed living out his last days.

To say that the strike was disruptive of the average New Yorker's everyday life would be a gross understatement. People carpooled, walked, and used whatever mass transit routes were running. For Bronx residents, this meant the New York Central (now

TWU pickets at City Hall. The hatless gray-haired man third from left is Douglas MacMahon, a TWU vice president who took over negotiations when Michael Quill was jailed. Next to McMahon is Shirley Quill, the TWU leader's wife. TWU Local 100 archives

Metro-North) commuter services on the Harlem and Hudson Lines, which paralleled subway routes in the central and western Bronx. Queens residents tried to squeeze aboard Long Island Rail Road (LIRR) trains at its various stations and also had a single bus route along Queens Boulevard (Green Bus Lines Q60) whose drivers were not TWU members and therefore continued to work. Staten Island residents still had the Staten Island Rapid Transit trains and their true lifeline, the ferry between St. George and Whitehall Street. Rail commuters departing from Penn Station and Grand Central in the afternoon peak found themselves herded into outdoor waiting areas in order to maintain an orderly passenger flow onto trains.

The experience of the New York Central Railroad with its Bronx train service sheds additional light on how hardy New York commuters coped with the strike. Its two lines, the Hudson and Harlem, under normal circumstances had a small cadre of three thousand regular commuters at fourteen stations from 138th Street to Riverdale and Wakefield, respectively. These riders were willing to pay $1 per ride for single tickets or $24 for a monthly, primarily to avoid the crowding of rush hour subway travel. During the strike, Bronx ridership mushroomed to 33,000, a twelvefold increase.

A group of innovative New York Central managers used barricades, signs, and colored tape to direct their sudden new customers to the right train when departing Grand Central. Police personnel, both from the railroad itself and New York City's police force, were essential to maintain order. Riders were lined up outside and admitted in groups to allow trains to load and depart safely. Fares were collected in large barrels supervised by the railroad's normal trainmen, accepting cash or valid tickets. It was challenging and difficult, but it worked.[3] There were no reported injuries, and riders moved between Grand Central and the New York Central's Bronx stations. If not comfortably, at least they got

3. From anecdotal observations of a now-retired New York Central railroad manager who later worked with the author at the LIRR.

TWU pickets at Manhattan's Civil Jail, where Quill was briefly incarcerated before being transferred to Bellevue Hospital after he suffered a heart attack. TWU Local 100 archives

Conferring during negotiations are Theodore Kheel (mediator), John Lindsay (mayor), Nathan Feinsinger (mediator), and unidentified man. TWU Local 100 archives

there. A newspaper account of how residents in one Bronx apartment building, in the vicinity of Morris Avenue and 183rd Street, coped with the strike noted that some people walked thirty minutes to a New York Central rail station, presumably University Heights on the Hudson Line or 183rd Street on the Harlem Line.[4]

Thankfully there were no major snowstorms during the strike, although Thursday January 6 was a rainy day. Some of the most innovative transit routes involved using New Jersey as a stepping stone. Rail passengers arriving at Grand Central or Penn Station who worked in Lower Manhattan used PATH trains between 33rd Street/Sixth Avenue and the Hudson Terminal (today's World Trade Center) Stations, by traveling to Jersey City and then back to New York. Upper Manhattan and West Bronx residents took New Jersey buses from the George Washington Bridge Bus Station to North Bergen, New Jersey, where they transferred to a second bus. Midtown travelers could then go directly to the Port Authority Bus Terminal at 41st Street and Eighth Avenue. Lower Manhattan travelers took the second bus to Hoboken, where a PATH train completed the trip.[5] In an additional twist, bus commuters from Bergen County, New Jersey, and Rockland County, New York, who normally took buses to the George Washington Bridge Bus Station in Washington Heights, opted instead to take buses to the Port Authority Bus Terminal.

The strike dragged on until Thursday morning, January 13. When it was finally settled the TWU gained its most important demands—a 15 percent wage increase and additional benefits, such as a $500 supplemental annual pension for retired workers.

4. *New York Times* (January 4, 1966).
5. *New York Times* (January 7, 1966).

Michael Quill (seated left), Nathan Feinsinger (seated right), and unidentified man conferring during negotiations. TWU Local 100 archives

The strike is over as the first bus, a B-10/New Lots Avenue run, leaves East New York Depot. The driver is Joseph Lindsay, no relation to the new mayor. TWU Local 100 archives

Once the drama over and Michael Quill's jailing and hospitalization settled down, a settlement was finally hammered out between Monday and Wednesday (January 10–12) of the second week. By this time the key players had changed. TWU Vice President Douglas MacMahon replaced the hospitalized Quill. Theodore Kheel replaced an ill Nathan Feinsinger as the chairman of the mediation panel, and Lindsay's deputy mayor, Robert Price, took on an active role. The new agreement was finally reached early in the morning of Thursday, January 13. Buses resumed before dawn, the first one on Brooklyn's B10 New Lots Avenue line, with one Joseph Lindsay at the wheel. An additional irony besides his surname was also noted when the *New York Times* reported that this particular Mr. Lindsay had been a tank driver when he was in military service. Subways took some hours to get back into service as not only the trains themselves but the signals, lighting, ventilation systems, and stations all had to be checked and secured before service could resume. Also trains were stored in the tunnels and had to be moved to terminals before service could resume. Despite the size of the system, full train service was running by the afternoon rush hour on January 13.[6]

Quill was eventually released from the hospital after the strike ended, and of course basked in the settlement he secured for his members and over Mayor Lindsay. Unfortunately Quill had all of two weeks to savor his strike victory, which indeed was his last hurrah. His heart condition still unimproved, he died at home on January 28.

The final irony occurred when Quill's funeral was held at St. Patrick's Cathedral on February 1. That day unionized hearse drivers in New York were on strike, but their

6. *New York Times* (January 14, 1966).

The final settlement is signed. Daniel Scannell (seated, right), a NYCTA board member, is next to TWU Local 100 President Matthew Guinan. TWU Local 100 archives

union, Teamsters Local 643, provided a driver working without pay and a station wagon, since hearses were unavailable. After the funeral Quill's corpse was driven to Gate of Heaven Cemetery in Westchester for burial. An era in New York history had truly ended.

Half a century after it occurred, memories of the 1966 strike may be faded, but those who experienced it know that it was a classic case of an event occurring that was never supposed to occur. While there have been two other general transit strikes since 1966 (in 1980 and 2005), the 1966 strike will be remembered much longer because it marked the end of one man's tenure and the beginning of another. It also set the stage for the significantly improved wages and benefits that all New York City municipal employees won during the eight years of Mayor Lindsay's tenure at City Hall. When a similar strike was threatened two years later, the TWU and the Transit Authority reverted to the old pattern and reached an agreement in the wee hours of New Year's Day. Chapter 20 gives more details of the January 1968 settlement.

19

1967: The BMT and IND Marry Forever

On November 26, 1957, ground was broken, at the corner of Chrystie and Canal Streets in Manhattan, on the biggest post–World War II subway construction project up to that time. Known as the Chrystie Street Connection, it was a pair of double-track tunnels connecting the IND south of Broadway Lafayette Station with the BMT tracks crossing the Manhattan and Williamsburg Bridges. Although no one knew it at the time, the finished Chrystie Street Connection would see its first revenue train exactly ten years later (November 26, 1967), well beyond its original target (car shortages were the primary reason behind the delayed opening).

Once opened, the project had lasting effects all over the IND and BMT divisions. Today it is recognized as an important milestone in the subway system's history because it allows alternate travel paths for many train routes. Chrystie Street's most important result was to increase service flexibility between southern Brooklyn and Midtown Manhattan by allowing BMT trains to use either the BMT Broadway trunk or the IND Sixth Avenue trunk north of the Manhattan Bridge. This flexibility has become increasingly important in the twenty-first century as reconstruction projects on the system require weekend or overnight closures of entire line segments. The alternate routings between Manhattan and Brooklyn reduce inconvenience when line segments must be closed for repair work.

First, a little background. When construction began on the original IND subway in 1925, its engineers made the momentous decision to build the IND physically compatible with the already-existing BMT subway—ten-foot-wide cars sixty-seven feet in length, requiring wider curves than IRT tunnels required. The advantage would be larger carrying capacity of the BMT cars, compared to the cramped dimensions on the IRT—fifty-one feet long and 8.5 feet wide. The long-term vision was to unite the BMT with the IND at strategic points so that trains could run in through services between the Bronx, or Queens, or Upper Manhattan, in the north, and Brooklyn in the south, traversing Mid-Manhattan in the process.[1]

1. IRT cars are fifty-one feet long and 8.5 feet wide, dimensions unchanged from the original 1904 subway. BMT's standard cars were sixty-seven feet long and ten feet wide; IND's original cars were sixty feet long and ten feet wide, but this dimension was compatible with BMT routes. After 1940,

The Chrystie Street Connection is actually five interconnected pieces that stretch from DeKalb Avenue in Brooklyn to 57th Street and Sixth Avenue. Going south to north, the first piece was the massive reconstruction of the BMT tracks between DeKalb Avenue and the Manhattan Bridge's Brooklyn portal, to simplify the track layout and eliminate a number of at-grade track crossings in that area. This work was completed in 1962, allowing the future new service patterns to be accommodated. Second and third were the two pairs of tunnels under Chrystie Street. The first pair links the IND Broadway-Lafayette Station express tracks with the BMT Manhattan Bridge's north side tracks and includes a station at Grand and Chrystie Streets. The second pair of tunnels join Broadway-Lafayette's local tracks with the BMT Williamsburg Bridge tracks and is known as the Essex Street Connector.

The fourth Chrystie Street piece is two low-level express tracks on the Sixth Avenue IND route between 34th and West 4th Street Stations, bridging a gap that had only two tracks because of the preexisting Hudson and Manhattan Railroad tunnels (today's PATH system) under Sixth Avenue when the IND was built in 1936–1940. The fifth piece is a two-track extension of the Sixth Avenue IND local tracks northward from 47th–50th Street Stations to a new terminal station at 57th Street (in 1989 this was connected to the 63rd Street Tunnel). The second and fourth pieces opened November 26, 1967; the third and fifth pieces on July 1, 1968.

The justification for this project was to enable the BMT and IND divisions to merge their services between Brooklyn and Manhattan and reduce imbalances between both divisions. The BMT Broadway Line carried three of the four major routes between Manhattan and Coney Island—the Brighton, Sea Beach, and West End services, which crossed the Manhattan Bridge on its north side. The tracks on the Manhattan Bridge south side were used less intensely and carried weekday local services between Lower Manhattan and the West End and Brighton Lines, by connecting to the Nassau Street subway. The IND Sixth Avenue trunk only carried the Culver Line. The overburdened Broadway BMT on the Manhattan Bridge north side may have contributed to the structural problems that periodically closed those tracks in the 1980s, 1990s, and early 2000s.

By permitting both the IND Sixth Avenue and BMT Broadway line access to and from the Manhattan Bridge, a more balanced track utilization could occur. After November 1967 Sixth Avenue trains used the north side and Broadway trains used the south side; the connection between Nassau Street and the south side was severed. A more balanced service pattern was initially established, with Brighton and West End

---

when all three systems were unified under Board of Transportation control, new cars built for both the BMT and IND continued using the IND's dimensions. While some car models built in the 1970s and 1980s (R44, R46, and R68) are seventy-five feet by ten feet, more recent car orders (R143 and R160 models) have gone back to sixty feet by ten.

Looking south on Chrystie Street from approximately Delancey Street, the Chrystie Street Connection is under construction, near the future Grand Street Station, in December 1961. A pile driver is pounding station support beams into the ground. NYTM

April 1958, looking northwest from a point above Sara Delano Roosevelt Park, with Forsythe Street in the foreground and Chrystie Street in the background. Track connection to enable Williamsburg Bridge trains to access the new route is under construction. Today M trains use this route. NYTM

Intersection of Delancey and Chrystie Streets during construction. NYTM

In October 1958, construction proceeds below Chrystie Street. NYTM

trains operating on the north side to and from Sixth Avenue; Sea Beach and additional Brighton Line rush hour services used the south side.

Another key improvement was that the Williamsburg Bridge services would for the first time have a direct route to Midtown Manhattan, eliminating the need to transfer at Essex and Delancey Streets or at Canal Street.

The Chrystie Street project goes back to at least 1949 when the Board of Transportation proposed it as part of the overall Second Avenue plan. In 1951 city voters approved a $500 million bond issue to fund the Second Avenue Subway, which included the connections at Chrystie Street. As already noted, on November 26, 1957, actual construction began on

Installation of new signal equipment is underway for the Chrystie Street Connection. NYTM

Work proceeds to finish the Grand Street Station. Neither tracks nor third rail have been installed yet. NYTM

Street-level entrance to the new Grand Street Station. Photo is looking west along Grand Street, with Chrystie Street running across the back. NYTM

The April 1961 groundbreaking ceremony for the lower-level express tracks below Sixth Avenue (Avenue of the Americas) between West 4th and 34th Street stations. Chairman Charles Patterson is the man second from left, holding the shovel. This project was part of the entire DeKalb–Chrystie–Sixth Avenue project and also opened in November 1967. NYTM

the Chrystie Street link. The groundbreaking for the lower-level tracks under Sixth Avenue was held on April 19, 1961.

As often happens with this type of construction, unexpected challenges occur without warning. Beginning in January 1962 residents of the neighborhood along Sixth Avenue, specifically the owners of a new luxury rental apartment at 13th Street, attempted to stop the overnight blasting work and succeeded, in August 1962, in forcing the contractor to stop working between 11 PM and 8 AM. Then in October 1962, the same week

A train of R32 cars stops at Grand Street shortly after the new connection opened in November 1967. It is either a B or D train. NYTM

as the Cuban Missile Crisis, blasting for the lower-level tunnels under Sixth Avenue at 24th Street caused an undermining of a bedrock cushion between the PATH tunnels, near the street surface, and the new tunnel being dug eighty feet underground. For five days PATH had to suspend service on its 33rd Street line while contractors for the NYCTA pumped over one thousand cubic yards of concrete into the excavation for the new tunnel, in order to prevent any future cave-in. A few weeks later, on December 7, a water main break at 18th Street and Sixth Avenue forced suspension of all subway and PATH service along that stretch for five more days. While the new subway construction did not cause the water main break, the service impacts were worse than during the October emergency and halted work on the new subway until December 24 to prevent any cave-in of the new tunnel. The service suspension also required IND trains to use a collection of temporary and unusual train routings for about a week. The D train was shifted to the Eighth Avenue Line between 59th and West 4th Streets, although its north (205th Street) and south (Coney Island) terminals were unchanged. A new, temporary DD Local train ran between the same two termini in lieu of the normal CC Local service between the Concourse Line and Hudson Terminal (today's World Trade Center). A second new service, the C train, ran express between Bedford Park Blvd and 34th Street, also replacing the BB and CC trains.

Then, on January 17, 1963, the prime contractor, Maclean-Grove-Shepherd Construction Company, halted all work because of unexpected higher costs and construction difficulties, specifically the ban on night work and damage from the water main break. The contractor asked for additional compensation; NYCTA told the firm to file for the additional costs when the project was completed. The contractor rejected this idea; the matter went before the New York City Corporation Counsel. The problem was finally resolved later in July 1963 when the city agreed to pay 90 percent of cost over-runs and the contractor the remaining 10 percent.

Construction began in February 1964 on the final piece, the two-track stub from 52nd to 58th Streets below Sixth Avenue to provide a terminal station for trains originating in Brooklyn. During that year Sixth Avenue was torn up for the new tunnel excavation because it was built close to the street surface; by early 1965 the street was covered in temporary decking so that traffic could move while the work continued underneath.

Finally, after many target dates to begin the new Chrystie Street services were announced and then revised, November 26, 1967, became the opening date, the Sunday after Thanksgiving. Ten days prior, the service changes were announced in the newspapers. The key changes would affect BMT routes between southern Brooklyn and Midtown Manhattan. The BMT Brighton Line was merged into the IND Sixth Avenue Concourse Line, with the new service using the "D" train designation from the IND; that letter would still designate a route between Coney Island and 205th Street, but it would now travel via the Manhattan Bridge and the Brighton Beach Line. Similarly, the BMT West End route married the IND's Sixth Avenue–Washington Heights Local and used a new "B" train designation. The "RR" Fourth Avenue local was rerouted to run 24/7 between 95th Street/Bay Ridge and Astoria, which was its terminal between 1949 and 1961. A new "EE" service was created to operate weekdays between Forest Hills and Whitehall Street (on the BMT Broadway Line) to replace the previous "RR" route in Queens and Manhattan. On the Broadway BMT trunk line, a new "QB" rush hour Brighton Line express-local service was created between 57th Street and Coney Island. Finally, a rush-hour-only express, the "NX" train between Brighton Beach, Coney Island, and Midtown was created using the N route's unused express tracks between Coney Island and 59th Street, Brooklyn, running nonstop between those two stops and giving residents of the many new apartment complexes in the Brighton Beach and Coney Island areas a faster trip to Manhattan than was previously possible. This meant that for the first time Stillwell Avenue–Coney Island would be an intermediate stop, not a terminal.

There were additional changes on IND and BMT routes. The F line, which operated between 179th Street/Jamaica and either 34th Street/Sixth Avenue or Broadway-Lafayette Streets in Manhattan, was extended all the way to Coney Island via the Culver Line route to became a 24/7 replacement for the D train. The Broadway-Brooklyn/ Jamaica Avenue elevated, up to this time the #14 and #15 trains, was provided with three separate services, JJ, QJ, and RJ. The first was the basic off-peak and weekend service between Broad Street and 168th Street–Jamaica; the second one was a weekday-only service between Coney Island and 168th Street–Jamaica. In rush hours the JJ provided a supplemental service between Canal Street and Atlantic Avenue; it was originally the Broadway Short Line (old #14). The RJ was a rush-hour-only service between 95th Street–Brooklyn and 168th Street–Jamaica, designed to supplement the RR and QJ lines. The QJ and RJ replaced the BMT's so-called Banker's Special trains that ran in rush hours between Lower Manhattan and the Fourth Avenue and Brighton Lines.

Many people were returning to work from a four-day Thanksgiving weekend on Monday November 27 when the new service impacts really kicked in. To say that confusion reigned on that first morning would be an understatement. Thousands of riders were on routes that were unfamiliar. One motorman on the new D train route punched the wrong route request button at Atlantic Avenue and ended up taking his train to Canal Street, where it was not supposed to go.[2]

New York Times (November 28, 1967).

After some weeks riders settled into the new patterns, but not without the usual criticisms that often accompany systemwide changes. Brighton Line riders, used to traveling though Manhattan on the Broadway BMT route, never became completely used to the new pattern. Finally, in 1999, at the time of another major service adjustment, the

New York Times (November 28, 1967).

2. *New York Times* (November 28, 1967).

pre–Chrystie Street Q train was resurrected to give Brighton Line riders 24/7 service between Coney Island and 57th Street/Seventh Avenue, restoring the historical BMT route.

Other changes were made in 1968. On April 12, the much-heralded NX train ran its last trip, having lasted not even six months. It died from lack of ridership. Customers from Brighton Beach and Ocean Parkway did not flock to the new service because the NX moniker apparently confused them into thinking that the train was a Sea Beach Line service making local stops. Operationally the train created headaches for train dispatchers and supervisors because signal constraints limited its effectiveness. Between Eighth Avenue and Kings Highway, only one train at a time could operate because the Sea Beach express tracks did not have block signals at that time. Threading the train through Stillwell Avenue terminal was also a potential headache.

The other 1968 changes related to the Chrystie Street project had an interesting history. On July 1 the Sixth Avenue line's one-station extension to 57th Street opened, along with the Essex Street Connector between Broadway-Lafayette Station and the Williamsburg Bridge tracks. A new service dubbed KK was created to operate between 57th Street/Sixth Avenue and 168th Street/Jamaica Avenue, encompassing the IND subway and the BMT elevated route through Brooklyn and Queens. This service was assigned IND R9 cars that were given some cosmetic fixes (fiberglass seats and repainting). NYCTA hoped that this service would take some customers from the overcrowded E and F trains originating in Jamaica, and it also would create a one-seat travel path to Midtown Manhattan for customers along the Broadway elevated in Bushwick and Williamsburg. The KK route, later simply the K, never lived up to its early hype and stopped running in 1976. For the next thirty-four years only nonrevenue train moves used the Essex Street Connector, but in 2010 it was once again raised to revenue train status when the M train was rerouted to connect the BMT's old Eastern Division to the IND Sixth Avenue subway. This time, the new service through the Essex Connector was widely praised and will no doubt continue for a long time.

In August 1968 the Chrystie Street routings were given a final tweak: the D train's south terminal became Brighton Beach weekdays between 6 AM and 8 PM, and the QJ train was extended to Coney Island.

The terminal station at 57th Street was, in turn, physically connected to the 63rd Street Tunnel in the early 1970s as part of the MTA's 1968 "Program for Action," a comprehensive list of capital projects that were made public on March 1, 1968, the day the MTA took over NYCTA. It was not until 1989 that revenue trains began using this linkage, which permitted trains to travel as far north as 21st Street–Queensbridge in Long Island City In late 2001, thanks to a new flying junction built just north of Queens Plaza, F trains were switched to this newer routing between 47th–50th Streets and Roosevelt Avenue–Jackson Heights, in lieu of the original 53rd Street Tunnel travel path in use since 1940.

20

1968: The MTA Is Created and Express Buses Appear

The year 1968 saw major political upheavals in the United States. The Vietnam War, a burning issue since 1965, toppled President Lyndon Johnson from office when he announced to the nation on March 31 that "I will not seek, and will not accept, the nomination of my party for another term as your president." Five days later, Martin Luther King Jr. was assassinated. Robert F. Kennedy, running for the Democratic Presidential nomination, was assassinated on June 5. Republican Richard Nixon emerged as the narrow winner in a presidential election that was a bitter, three-way race against the Democratic candidate, Vice President Hubert Humphrey, and the third-party candidate, George Wallace, Alabama's past and future governor, running on a "law and order" platform.

It was also a watershed year in the history of the New York City bus and subway system. As Chapter 10 recounted, in 1953 the New York City Transit Authority was created under New York State law, taking direct control of the subways and publicly owned buses from New York City's mayor to an independent agency governed by its own board. This arrangement worked reasonably well, with only one fare increase from 1953 until 1966.

After the 1966 transit strike was settled, Mayor John Lindsay was able to focus on implementing his initiatives for the city's government, including a 1965 campaign promise to use the surplus toll revenues from the Triborough Bridge and Tunnel Authority (TBTA) to offset the NYCTA's deficits. This proposal ran afoul of TBTA Chairman Robert Moses, a man with strong pro-auto and anti-transit biases. Moses branded the Lindsay proposal "illegal." Mayor Lindsay's new transportation chief, Arthur Palmer, conferred with Moses about the proposal only to be lectured by the venerable Moses about the illegalities of the idea. A lobbying trip to Albany to convince state legislators to pass laws permitting such a fund transfer was thwarted when the hearing was packed with Moses supporters testifying for the continuation of the status quo.[1]

At the same time, Governor Nelson Rockefeller was looking to put his imprint on the region's transportation systems. Despite their public personas as like-minded lib-

---

1. Vincent Cannato, *The Ungovernable City* (New York: Basic Books, 2001), 96.

eral Republicans, privately they disliked each other and each viewed the other as a rival. Both had higher political ambitions (read: president). Both would vie for behind-the-scenes control of the city's mass transit. Rockefeller would emerge triumphant; Lindsay would not.

In 1965, prior to Lindsay's election to City Hall, Rockefeller pushed through state legislation that created a Metropolitan Commuter Transportation Authority (MCTA), a new public agency designed to own and operate the Long Island Rail Road once that carrier was taken out of the private sector. In January 1966, right after Lindsay's election, New York State formally purchased the LIRR from its corporate parent, the once-massive Pennsylvania Railroad. The state was now in the transportation business in a big way.

Rockefeller, as he did with many other issues, always thought big. He saw the difficulty that the mayor was having in capturing the TBTA surpluses for transit use, decided the time was ripe to create a new, umbrella-like state transportation agency that would expand the MCTA beyond the LIRR, and give it oversight of the NYCTA and TBTA as well. The bridge and tunnel toll surpluses would be available for transit subsidies, and the governor would emerge the savior. Part of the changeover would see the MCTA be rechristened as the Metropolitan Transportation Authority, or MTA.

The whole changeover started with the New York State legislature passing new amendments to the state's public authorities law that created a Metropolitan Transportation District and the MTA to be in charge. Naturally Governor Rockefeller signed the bill for the benefit of news photographers. More important, Rockefeller tied the MTA's creation to a $2.5 billion transportation bond issue that would require voters to approve it in the November 1967 election. Rockefeller even campaigned personally for the bond issue in a year when there were no important statewide or federal positions on the ballot—the transportation bonds were *the* issue in 1967. Of the total $2.5 billion of bonds, $1.25 billion was earmarked for improvements to the state's mass transit systems. The biggest chunk would go to New York City and the seven New York counties surrounding it—Nassau, Suffolk, Westchester, Putnam, Dutchess, Rockland, and Orange. NYCTA, LIRR, the New York Central Railroad, the New Haven Railroad (both of which are now Metro-North), and the Staten Island Railway would all benefit if the bonds passed.[2]

In a show of bipartisan unity that would be unheard of in Washington in the twenty-first century, most of the state's elected officials, regardless of party affiliation, supported the bonds. The day before the actual election, two brand-new R40 cars were displayed on the IND tracks at 34th Street and Sixth Avenue. Inside the cars Governor Rockefeller, Mayor Lindsay, and City Council President Frank O'Connor were photo-

2. NYS Public Authorities Law, §1260.

graphed together. Indeed, the bond issue passed by a three-to-two vote, and the MTA was primed to replace its smaller predecessor early in 1968.

Before that could occur, there was the matter of the NYCTA's expiring contract with the TWU, the one hammered out after the twelve-day strike two years earlier. Eager to avoid another showdown, NYCTA and the TWU reached an agreement right before the New Year's morning deadline. A new contract with another substantial wage increase was signed.[3] Unlike the situation of two years' prior, Mayor Lindsay was pictured smiling on the front page of the *Times* on New Year's Day, and a headline proclaimed, "Mayor Is Praised for Transit Role."[4] The TWU leadership was also quick to praise the mayor. One reason was that the 1968 contract also gave NYCTA workers (and later, all MTA employees) the ability to retire with approximately half-pay after twenty years of service if the employee were fifty years of age or over. Soon this provision would have major effects on the subways and, beyond that, for the entire MTA family, as large numbers of skilled and knowledgeable employees left to take advantage of this new benefit.

New York Times (January 2, 1968).

In the meantime, the MTA changeover occurred on March 1, 1968. As that date dawned, the MTA assumed oversight for NYCTA, the LIRR, the two commuter railroad operations that became Metro-North, and the TBTA. With the MTA's creation, Governor Rockefeller emerged as the top transportation dog in New York, relegating Mayor Lindsay to the sidelines.

Another transportation development that occurred in 1968 was the introduction of significant express bus services between Manhattan and outlying boroughs. Green Bus Lines began a single such route in June 1962, to replace discontinued Long Island Rail

3. *New York Times* (January 2, 1968).
4. *New York Times* (January 2, 1968).

Road service between Ozone Park and Penn Station. A few years later, Henry Barnes, the city's independent-minded traffic commissioner, suggested additional such routes to tap areas without direct subway access. Barnes's suggestion led to three new express routes started in 1968 on an experimental basis. Ultimately, they became the embryo of a larger system that has continued to grow in the last forty-plus years.

Steinway Transit Corporation, a long-time Queens private operator, started the first 1968 express bus route on February 26, between Fresh Meadows and Midtown Manhattan. The second route started August 19 between Riverdale, the Bronx, and Midtown; this time a brand-new private company, Riverdale Transit was the operator (its management was connected to private commuter bus operators in New Jersey). New York City Transit Authority jumped on the express bandwagon on December 9, when its first route between Staten Island and Manhattan was opened for business; this one had branches to both Lower and Midtown Manhattan. In all cases the routes were originally deemed experimental; that moniker quickly disappeared as both the Transit Authority and the private companies continued to add routes and buses well into the 1980s. In 2005–2006, when the MTA took over the city's remaining private bus companies, the express bus routes were included. A service that was once started to compete with the subways has become a complement to the subways.

LOOKING BACK

The 1940–1968 period is memorable for many historic events, both transit specific and global. In New York, mass transit began its slow but inevitable metamorphosis from the private sector to the public sector. Prior to 1940, only the IND subway was publicly owned and operated. In 1940, after years of debate, New York City bought the IRT and BMT companies and unified the subway system under the Board of Transportation's management. Between 1940 and 1962, 80 percent of the city's streetcars and buses were absorbed by the Board of Transportation or its 1953 successor, the New York City Transit Authority. Except for Brooklyn's streetcars and buses, the public takeovers in the other four boroughs occurred without much prior warning. By 1968, when the Metropolitan Transportation Authority was created, its short-lived predecessor, the Metropolitan Commuter Transportation Authority, had also taken the Long Island Rail Road into the public sector, sowing the beginning of what has become the largest regional transportation provider in North America. By then it was recognized everywhere in the United

R40 subway car, the last model ordered by and delivered to NYCTA before it became part of the Metropolitan Transportation Authority. The sloped-end design was not successful and was even modified on the last hundred cars of this order to resemble the R42, the next order. Of the four hundred total R40 cars delivered, the final two hundred were equipped with factory air conditioning. NYTM

A new R42 consist, the first car order to carry the MTA's new "Big M" logo. NYTM

The first NYCTA express bus route to/from Manhattan, the R9X, serving Great Kills Staten Island, debuts on December 9, 1968. NYTM

In the MTA's second year, exact fare payment became a requirement on all buses as a deterrent to robberies and assaults. This B41/Flatbush Avenue bus was photographed a few days after the requirement was put into effect. It also displays the new MTA logo. NYTM

In July 2003, the R36 subway cars, originally bought for the 1964 World's Fair, were running their final miles. The LIRR M3 consist pictured was still in service in 2014. Both display the MTA's more recent "Pac-Man" logo. Author's photograph

States and Canada that mass transit is a vital public service that must receive taxpayer support in addition to the fares that users pay.

Whether the Board of Transportation, the independent New York City Transit Authority, or the MTA–New York City Transit Authority was in charge of the subways and buses, its critics were always more visible than its allies. Regardless, the fact is that during this twenty-eight-year period significant progress was made to improve a system that had been ravaged by a prior lack of investment in infrastructure and the wear and tear caused by heavy World War II ridership.

On the subway side, over 5,800 new cars were purchased and placed in service between 1947 and 1968, replacing virtually all pre–World War II IRT and BMT equipment as well as significant amounts of IND stock from the early 1930s. But the subway improvements hardly ended with the cars themselves. Many stations had their platforms lengthened to accommodate ten-car trains, even on the local services. Signals, many of which dated to the early 1900s, were replaced with more modern and reliable hardware. Fluorescent platform lighting was installed all over the system. Free transfer points between divisions were created beginning in 1948 to improve travel flexibility.

An ambitious new routes program was proposed in the early 1950s, partially funded by a $500 million bond issue that voters approved in 1951. The funds would have built the Second Avenue Subway and connections to it in Queens and the Bronx, as well as additional routes in Brooklyn. These new lines did not come to pass, but significant new route miles were added between 1941 and 1967, as documented in this book. Chapter 3 covered how the Bronx's Dyre Avenue Line was merged into the subway system from an abandoned railroad route. Chapter 12 described three instances of the IND and BMT merging. The IND Fulton Street was extended from Brooklyn into Queens using part of an older BMT elevated, which also allowed it to provide a new service to the Rockaway Peninsula using an old Long Island Rail Road route. Two more short but strategic track connections in Brooklyn and Queens allowed additional IND and BMT services to integrate. Chapter 19 covered the final, official merging of those two divisions in November 1967 when the Chrystie Street Connection and its associated new tunnels and rebuilt lines in Brooklyn and Manhattan became reality. While the delay in building the Second Avenue route is only now being rectified, it is recognized that spending the funds first on some key connecting tracks and upgrading the basic infrastructure of the entire system was wiser than building entirely new routes.

On the noncapital side, November 1967 is also significant because Chrystie Street's opening also inaugurated the official first rollout of today's universal means of identifying trains and routes. Prior to then, IRT trains built after 1947 did carry number designations on their headsigns, but the numbers did not appear on official subway maps. The IND division's letter designations were certainly public knowledge. BMT trains were beginning to use letter designations to replace an older set of numbered route monikers, but in both cases official maps did not display either division's route identifiers.

The official subway map issued in November 1967 included these designations for the first time—IRT route numbers and BMT-IND letters that reflected an extension of the IND's original identifiers. Maps also eliminated the old three-division color code (blue for IRT, red for IND, and yellow for BMT) in favor of showing each route as a separate and distinct line, which meant that some colors had to be repeated. That nomenclature was later replaced with a more logical system that uses a unique color for each Manhattan-based trunk line; this is still in use today. More important, as of November 1967 the IRT, IND, and BMT ceased to exist officially. Since then the former IRT is the A Division, and the IND-BMT is the B Division.

A final word here about the surface lines. The private bus operators that came into the public-sector fold in 1947, 1948, and 1962 were all situations when sudden crises, either financial or labor driven, forced private companies to cede their operations on short notice. The result was that the Board of Transportation or New York City Transit Authority inherited motley and worn-out bus fleets. Between 1956 and 1968 over 3,500 new buses, all forty-foot diesel-powered vehicles, were placed in service in all five boroughs. The first buses equipped with air conditioning appeared in 1967. Express buses, a premium fare service aimed at residents without direct subway access in the Bronx, Queens, and Staten Island, first appeared in 1968.

For many New Yorkers, the most memorable difference between the pre- and post-1968 era was the introduction of air-conditioned subway cars. An experimental group of six cars, part of a normal ten-car consist on the F train, was successfully tested in the summer of 1967. The result was that in December of that year, the *New York Times* featured a front-page article with the headline "600 Subway Cars to Have Air Conditioning by 1969."[5] An item that is now taken for granted was very big news when the first production-line models of the new, cool cars arrived in September 1968.

5. *New York Times* (December 3, 1967).

And so it goes. Big news yesteryear is barely a yawn today. The subway has always been the highway of the masses, its fare closely tracking the cost of a slice of pizza. While no one wants to buy a cold pizza slice, a cold subway ride in the summer represented to most people the most important change between 1940 and 1968.

Bibliography

Cannato, Vincent J. *The Ungovernable City: John Lindsay and His Struggle to Save New York*. New York: Basic Books, 2001.

Caro, Robert. *The Power Broker: Robert Moses and the Fall of New York*. New York: Knopf, 1974.

Cudahy, Brian J. *Under the Sidewalks of New York: The Story of the World's Greatest Subway System*. New York: Fordham University Press, 1995.

———. *A Century of Subways—Celebrating One Hundred Years of New York's Underground Railways*. New York: Fordham University Press, 2003.

Derrick, Peter. *Tunneling to the Future—The Story of the Great Subway Expansion That Saved New York*. New York: New York University Press, 2001.

Federal Writers Project. *WPA Guide to New York City*. New York: Federal Writers Project, 1939.

Fischler, Stan. *Uptown, Downtown: A Trip Through Time on New York's Subways*. New York: Hawthorn, 1976.

———. *Confessions of a Trolley Dodger from Brooklyn*. Flushing, N.Y.: H&M Productions, 1995.

Fischler, Stan. *The Subway*. New York: H&M Productions, 1997.

Fischler, Stan, with John Henderson. *The Subway and the City: Celebrating a Century*. Syosset, N.Y.: Frank Merriwell, 2004.

Freeman, Joshua. *In Transit*. New York: Oxford University Press, 1989.

Garrett, Charles. *The LaGuardia Years: Machine and Reform Politics in New York City*. New Brunswick, N.J.: Rutgers University Press, 1961.

Greller, James C. *New York City Transit System Bus and Trolley Coach Fleet, 1946–1958*. West Orange, N.J.: Xplorer, n.d.

Greller, James C., and Edward Watson. *The Brooklyn Elevated*. Hicksville, N.Y.: NJ International, n.d.

Heckscher, August R., and Phyllis Robinson. *When LaGuardia Was Mayor: New York's Legendary Years*. New York: Norton, 1978.

Hood, Clifton. *722 Miles: The Building of the Subways and How They Transformed New York*. Baltimore, MD: Johns Hopkins University Press, 1993.

Jackson, Kenneth, ed. *Encyclopedia of New York City*. 2nd ed. New Haven, Conn.: Yale University Press, 2010.

Kaplan, Lawrence, and Carol P. Kaplan. *Between Ocean and City: The Transformation of Rockaway, New York*. New York: Columbia University Press, 2003.

Kramer, Frederick A. *Building the Independent Subway—The Technology and Intense Struggle of New York City's Most Gigantic Venture*. Quadrangle Press, 1990.

———. *Subway to the World's Fair*. Westfield, N.J.: Bells and Whistles, 1991.

———. *Third Avenue Railway*. Flanders, N.J.: RAE, 2001.

Metropolitan Transportation Authority. *Metropolitan Transportation—A Program For Action*. New York: MTA, February 1968.

Ogden, Oliver. *New York Fifth Avenue Coach Company, 1885–1960*. Hudson, Wis.: Iconografix, 2009.

Quill, Shirley. *Mike Quill, Himself: A Memoir*. Greenwich, Conn.: Devin-Adair, 1985.

Reed, Robert C. *The New York Elevated*. Cranbury, N.J.: A. S. Barnes, 1978.

Sansone, Gene. *New York Subways: An Illustrated History of New York City's Transit Cars*. Baltimore, Md.: Johns Hopkins University Press, 2004.

Whittemore, L. H. *The Man Who Ran the Subways: The Story of Mike Quill*. New York: Holt, Rinehart and Winston, 1968.

Fortune (July 1940)
Motor Coach Age (July 1971, July 1975)
New York Times
http://www.nycsubway.org.
http://www.thejoekorner.com/indexfrm.html.

Index

A Division, 165

air-conditioned buses, 92, *135*, 165

air-conditioned subway cars, 90, 139, 140, 141, *163*, 165

Amalgamated Association of Street Electric Railway and Motor Coach Employees of America, 83

Amalgamated Transit Union, 83, 86, 145

American Federation of Labor, 86

Atlantic Avenue elevated station, *44*

A train, 6, 103, 107, 108–9

B25/Fulton Street bus route, 8, *9*

B35 Church Avenue bus route, *35*

Banker's Special trains, 157

bankruptcy: Surface Transportation and, 41; Third Avenue Transit System and, 37–38

Barnes, Henry, 162

Baychester Avenue, *26*

Baychester Avenue Station, *28*

BB train, 155

B Division, 140, 165

Berger, Meyer, 82

Bianco, Carmen, 141

Bingham, Sidney H., 70, 81

"Bingham Macks," 58n6, 70–71

black transit workers, 22–24

BMT. *See* Brooklyn-Manhattan Transit Company

BMT Division: Chrystie Street Connection, 151–58, 165; formation of B Division, 140. *See also* Brooklyn-Manhattan Transit Company

Board of Transportation: 1947–1949 purchases of new buses, 38, 50, 55–56, 57–58, 68–70; 1947 bus and trolley operations in Queens, *52*; 1948 transit fare increase, 62–66; 1950 transit fare increase, 66; Chrystie Street Connection, 153; Dyre Avenue subway extension and, 27–28; elimination of Brooklyn elevated lines, 46–47, 75–79; elimination of the Third Avenue elevated, 111; fiscal and political problems plaguing, 80–81; historical overview, 1, 3; IND–BMT linkages, 100–101; Memorandum of Understanding with the TWU, 83; overview of transit changes from 1940 to 1968, 162–63, 164; postwar re-equipage of Brooklyn's trolleys, 67;

private to public bus transitions in Staten Island, Queens, and Manhattan, 49–58; purchase of R series subway cars, 89–90; replacement by the NYCTA, 80–81; responsibilities of, 1; streetcar-to-bus conversion, 8–9, 68–74; subway unification and, 1, 2, 11–12 (*see also* subway unification)

bond issues, 164

Boston Elevated Railway Company, 62

Brennan, James, 47

Breslin, Jimmy, 144

"Brightliner" subway cars, 141

Brighton Line, *72*, 152–53, 156, 157–58

Brighton Local, 107

Broadway-Brooklyn/Jamaica Avenue elevated, 78, 90, 156

Broadway–Kingsbridge streetcar, 36

Broadway-Lafayette Station, 152, 158

Broadway-Nassau Station, 70

Broadway–Seventh Avenue Express subway, 122–23

Broadway–Seventh Avenue Local subway, *55*, 122

Broadway Short Line, 157

Broadway subway (BMT), 151, 152

Bronx: 1948 transit fare increase and, 63; 1966 transit strike and, 146–47, 148; Dyre Avenue subway extension, *26*, 27–30; IND Concourse subway proposal, 26–27; streetcars, *32*, *40*; streetcar-to-bus conversion, 33, 36; Third Avenue elevated, 116

Bronx Hub, *116*

Brooklyn: 1948 transit fare increase and, 63; elevated lines, 4, 5, 42–48, 75–79; growth of following the Civil War, 42–43; steam railroad lines, 43, 45; streetcars, 7–8, 42–48, 67; streetcar-to-bus conversion, 6–10, 67–74

Brooklyn Bridge: cable car line, 42; elevated trains and trolleys, 6, 42–48, 75

Brooklyn-Manhattan Transit Company (BMT): Banker's Special trains, 157; B Division and, 165; Brooklyn elevated lines and, 4, 5; Brooklyn Rapid Transit Company and, 2–3, 75; Chrystie Street Connection, 151–58, 165; compatibility with the IND, 3, 100, 105–6, 151; Dual Contracts agreements and, 2; historical overview, 2–3;

Brooklyn-Manhattan Transit (*continued*)
identification of trains and routes, 165; IND–
BMT connections, 5–6, 90–91, 100–110, 151–58;
overview of transit changes from 1940 to 1968,
162, 164–65; Q type wooden elevated line cars, 79;
R series subway cars, 90, 106, 107; Standard Cars,
105–6; streetcars, 7–8; streetcar-to-bus conver-
sion, 6–10; subway car dimensions, 151; subway
unification and, 1, 3–4, 6–12; Transport Workers
Union and, 10; Triplex subway car, *14*; upgrading
issues, 11–12; World's Fair service, 14
Brooklyn Rapid Transit Company (BRT): Brooklyn-
Manhattan Transit Company and, 2–3, 75; Dual
Contracts agreements, 59, 60; elevated lines, 75;
founding of, 45; Slaughter Huff and, 35n5;
Standard Cars, 105–6
BRT. *See* Brooklyn Rapid Transit Company
B train, 156
Budd Company, 137, 139, 141, 142
buses: 1941 strike in Manhattan, 20–21; 1946 strike
against Isle Transportation, 50; 1955 NYCTA
plan for the privatization of, 87, 89; air-condi-
tioning, 92, *135*, 165; Board of Transportation's
1947–1949 bus purchases, 38, 50, 55–56, 57–58,
68–70; double-deck (*see* double-deck buses);
dual-powered, 33, *40*; elimination of the Third
Avenue elevated and, 115; express service
between Manhattan and outlying boroughs,
161–62, *163*; free transfers to a subway, *91*; Great
Northeast Blackout, 95; NYCTA's moderniza-
tion, *91*, 92–93; private to public transitions in
Staten Island, Queens, and Manhattan, 49–58;
Queens bus operations in 1947, *51*; streetcar-to-
bus conversion (*see* streetcar-to-bus conversion). *See also* Fifth Avenue Coach Company;
Fifth Avenue Coach Lines; Fifth Avenue Coach/
Surface Transit; General Motors Corporation
buses; Mack buses; New York City Omnibus
Corporation; Twin Coach Company buses;
Yellow Coach buses
bus fares: 1948 increase, 23, 62–66; 1949 increase, 23;
1950 increase, 66; financial problems of the
Surface Transportation System and, 37; Manhat-
tan fare increases, 23; Third Avenue Transit's
labor issues and, 38–39
BX1 bus route, 33, *118*
BX2 bus route, 33, *40*
BX27/Clason Point bus route, *41*
BX29/Willis Avenue bus route, *40*

cable car line: across the Brooklyn Bridge, 42
Canarsie Line, *91*, 107
carbon steel subway cars, 137
Casey, Hugh, 81
CC train, 155
Chalk, O. Roy, 130
Chicago, 94
Chicago Motor Coach, 16, 20, 96, 99, 117
Chicago Rapid Transit, 62
Chicago Surface Lines, 62
Chicago Transit Authority (CTA), 62, 80, 117
Chrystie Street Connection, 90, 91, 103, 151–58, 165
Church, Stanley, 28
Church Avenue Station, 101
Church Avenue streetcar, 71, 72, *73*
Cimillo, William, 39, 41
Citi Field, 138
Citizen's Budget Commission, 9
City Line (Brooklyn), 107. *See also* Fulton Street
elevated
civil service system: subway unification and, 10–11
Clancy, John T., *93*
closed shop, 19
Cohn, Roy M., 129, 130, 136
Cole, David, 145
collection shoes, 16n1
Committee of Fifteen, 61
Comprehensive Omnibus, 38, *55*, 56
Concourse–138th Street bus route, 33
Concourse–Hub bus route, 33
Concourse subway extension, 26–27
Condon–Wadlin Act, 145
conductors: on double-deck buses, 96–97
Coney Island: growth of, 43; steam railroads, 43, 45
Coney Island Avenue Line (streetcar), 71, 72
Coney Island Overhaul Facility, 141
Coney Island subway lines, 6
Coney Island Yard, *88*, 142
Congress of Industrial Organizations (CIO), 19
Connecticut Turnpike, 29
Contract One subway, 45n1
Contract Two subway, 45
Cortelyou Road line, 67, 68, 73
craft union model, 83–84, 86–87
Crosstown Bus Depot (Brooklyn), *146*
C train, 155
Culver, Andrew, 43
Culver Connection, 100, 101–2
Culver Line (elevated), 6, 43, 45, 73, 100

Culver Line (subway route), 101–2, 103, 106, 152
Culver Shuttle, 103
Curtayne, Vincent, 89

DD Local train, 155
DeKalb Avenue Station (Lexington Avenue El), 76
DeKalb Avenue streetcar, 44
DeKalb Avenue Junction (BMT subway), 90–91
Derrick, Peter, 60
Dewey, Thomas, 81
diesel buses, 33, 38. *See also* buses
diesel-electric buses, 33, *40*
Ditmas Avenue Station, 101, 102
double-deck buses: conversion to one-man buses,
    96–98; fares on, 17; first appearance of, 16;
    operated by Fifth Avenue Coach, *17, 18* (*see also*
    Fifth Avenue Coach Company); replacement with
    single-deck coaches, 98–99
double-ended streetcars, 35n5, 71
D train, 6, 102–3, 140, 155, 156, 158
Dual Contracts agreements, 2, 60, 111
Dual Contracts subways: replacement of elevated
    lines, 5. *See also* Brooklyn-Manhattan Transit
    Company (BMT); Independent Subway System;
    Interborough Rapid Transit Company (IRT):
dual-powered buses, 33, *40*
Dyre Avenue Line (subway extension), *26, 27*–30
Dyre Avenue Station, *30*

East 180th Street Station, *26*
East Side Omnibus Corporation, *32*, 38, 56
EE train, 107, 156
Eighty-Sixth Street Station, *125*
electric-powered surface transit vehicles. *See*
    streetcars and trolleys
Electric Railway President's Conference Committee, 7
elevated lines (els): across the Brooklyn Bridge,
    42–48; closing of Brooklyn's Lexington Avenue
    line, 75–79; development of, 4; elimination of the
    Third Avenue el, 111–16; linkages between BMT
    Brooklyn els and the IND subway network, 5–6;
    MUDC cars, 111; pressure to remove in the 1930s,
    4–5; wooden cars, 79. *See also* Fulton Street
    elevated
Eleventh Street Connection, 103–4, *104–5*
Essex Street Connector, 152, 158
E train, 105
Euclid Avenue Station, *105, 106*, 107
express buses, 161–62, *163, 165*

FACO Division (Fifth Avenue Coach), 117
Far Rockaway, 109
Far Rockaway/Mott Avenue station, *108*
Feinsinger, Nathan, 145, *148,* 149
Fifth Avenue Coach Company: becomes Fifth Avenue
    Coach Lines, 117; bus routes in the Bronx, 33;
    combined Fifth Avenue/NYCO operation, 8, 117
    (*see also* New York City Omnibus Corporation);
    conversion of double-deck buses to one-man
    operation, 96–98; fare increases, 23; history of, 16,
    17–18; labor relations, 18–24, 96–97; operation of
    double-deck buses, 16, *17, 18*; purchase of Mack
    C50 buses, 99; Queens bus operations in 1947, *52*;
    replacement of double-deck buses with single-
    deck coaches, 98–99; takeover of Third Avenue
    Transit, 31, 41, 117
Fifth Avenue Coach Lines: creation of, 117; GMC
    buses, *118, 119*; labor relations, 120–21; purchase
    of Surface Transportation, 41, 117; Surface
    Transit subsidiary, 117–21
Fifth Avenue Coach/Surface Transit: 1961 stock-
    holder suits, 129; 1962 seizure of garages and
    buses by New York City, 132–33, *134*; 1962 strikes,
    129–30, 131–32, *133*; later history of, 136; layoff of
    transit workers, 130–31; MABSTOA takeover,
    133–35; Harry Weinberg takeover, 129, 130–32, 135;
    Westchester Country routes, 135–36
Fifth Avenue elevated (Brooklyn), *43,* 45, 46
Fifth Avenue/Third Avenue elevated (Brooklyn),
    6, 111
Fifty-Ninth Street Station (Third Avenue Elevated), *113*
Fifty-Seventh Street Station, 158
Fifty-Third Street Station (Third Avenue Elevated), *112*
"Fishbowl" buses, *91, 92, 135*. *See also* "New Look"
    GM buses
five-cent fare. *See* nickel fare
Flatbush Avenue Line, *73*
Flushing–Ridgewood trolley line, 69, *73*
football games, 93–94
Fortune, 19–20
Fourth Avenue Local subway, 106, 107, 156
Freeman, Joshua, 19
F train, 6, 103, 105, 156, 158, 165
Fullen, William, 81
Fulton–Lexington elevated, 77
Fulton Street elevated, 6, 9, *43,* 45, 46, 77, 100,
    107–9, 111
Fulton Street Station, 70
Fulton Street subway, 45–46, 100, 107, 164

Garrett, Sylvester, 145

Gates Avenue Line (Brooklyn), *13*

General Motors Corporation (GMC) buses: "Fishbowl" buses, *91, 92, 135*; model 4506, 38, 55; model 4507, 38, *41*, 97, 98; model 4509, 97, 98, *99, 135*; model 4510, 55–56, 68, *69*, 72; model 5101, *54*, 56, 68, *69*, 70; model 5102, 98; model 5104, *98*, 99; model 5106, *54*; model 5301, 73, *135*; New Look buses, 73, *91, 92*; purchased by Fifth Avenue Coach, 8, *118, 119*; purchased by New York City Omnibus Corporation, 8, *118*; purchased by the Board of Transportation in 1948–1949, 38, 50, *52, 54*, 55–56, 68–70, *72*; Queen Mary double-deck buses, *17*, 96–98, *99*; in Third Avenue Transit's streetcar-to-bus conversion, 34, 38, *41. See also* Yellow Coach buses

Gordon, Mortimer, 38

Grand Central Station, 147, 148

Grand Street Station, *154*

Grant Avenue ramp, 107, 108–9

Grant Avenue station, 107

Great Northeast Blackout, 94–95

Green Bus Lines, *52*, 145, 147, 161–62

G train, 103

Guinan, Matthew, *83, 114, 150*

Gun Hill Road Station, *28*

Harlem Line (New York Central RR), 147

Harriman, Averill, 89

Hedley, Frank, 81

High Street–Brooklyn Bridge Station, 70

High Street subway, 48

"Hi-Speed Local" service, 123, *126*

Hodes, James, 37, 38

Hood, Clifton, 2

Hudson Line (New York Central RR), 147

Huff, Slaughter, 35, 37

"Huffliners," 35n5

Hylan, John, 3, 59

Impellitteri, Vincent, 81, 82

IND. *See* Independent Subway System

IND Division, 1, 140, 151–58, 165

Independent Subway System (IND): 1948 map of transfer privileges, *64*; B Division and, 140, 165; Chrystie Street Connection, 151–58, 165; compatibility with the BMT, 3, 100, 105–6, 151; Concourse subway proposal, 26–27; creation of, 3; Dyre Avenue subway extension and, 29; Fulton

Street subway, 45–46, 100, 107, 164; High Street subway-surface transfer, 48; identification of trains and routes, 165; IND–BMT connections, 5–6, 90–91, 100–110, 151–58, 164; labor relations issues, 10; linkages with BMT Brooklyn els, 5–6; nickel fare, 60; overview of transit changes from 1940 to 1968, 162, 164–65; Queens Boulevard subway, *93*; R series cars, *15*, 89–90, 106, 107, 158, 160; Second Phase, 27; service across Jamaica Bay, 109; subway car dimensions, 151; subway unification and, 1, 3–4; World's Fair service, 14–15

industrial union model, 82–83, 86–87

Interborough Rapid Transit Company (IRT): 1903 leasing of the Manhattan Railway network, 111; 1940 subway car fleet, 15; Broadway–Seventh Avenue Local, 55; Contract Two subway, 45; A Division and, 165; Dual Contracts agreements and, 2, 59, 60; Dyre Avenue subway extension and, 27, 28, 29, *30*; elimination of the Ninth Avenue and Second Avenue elevateds, 111; elimination of the Third Avenue elevated, 116; identification of trains and routes, 165; Manhattan elevated lines and, 4, 5; overview of transit changes from 1940 to 1968, 162; proposed route expansions in the 1950s, 90–91; R series subway cars, *88, 89*, 90, 116, 123; subway car dimensions, 151n1; subway unification and, 1, 3–4, 10–12; Transport Workers Union and, 10; upgrading issues, 11–12; West Side Improvement Project, 122–28; World's Fair subway service, 14, 137

intercompany transfers, 4

interdivisional transfers, 4

IRT. *See* Interborough Rapid Transit Company

Isaacs, Stanley M., 61

Isle Transportation Company, 49–50, *52*

Jamaica Avenue Line, *69*

Jamaica Bay, 109

Jamaica Buses, *52*

Jeffe, Ephraim, 81, 82

JJ train, 156–57

Johnson, Phyllis, *92, 93*

J train, 5, *13*, 90

Junction Boulevard Line, *69*

Kaufman, Samuel, 38

Kheel, Theodore, *83*, 86, 144–45, *148, 149*

KK train, 158

Klein, Harris, 82

labor relations: Fifth Avenue Coach Company and, 18–24, 96–97; Fifth Avenue Coach Lines and, 120–21; New York City Omnibus Corporation and, 18–24; NYCTA and, 82–87, 143–44, 161; Mike Quill's 1965 negotiations with John Lindsay, 144–45; subway unification and, 10–11; Third Avenue Railway Company and, 33–34; Third Avenue Transit System and, 38–39, 41; Robert F. Wagner and, 87, 143. *See also* strikes; transit workers; Transport Workers Union

LaGuardia, Fiorello: 1941 bus strike in Manhattan and, 21; attitude toward mass transit, 1–2; opposition to streetcars, 7, 8; pro-bus policy, 8, 9; streetcar-to-bus conversion and, 34–35; support for the nickel fare, 1–2, 12, 61; Transport Workers Union and, 11

Lehman, Herbert H., 11

Leonard, Frank, *104*

Leonard, Marie, *104*

Leslie, Joan, 36

Lexington Avenue #5 express, 25, 30

Lexington Avenue elevated (Brooklyn), 6, 45, 46, 75–79

Lexington Avenue subway, 25, 30, 75, 94, 116

Liberty Avenue elevated, 108–9

Liberty Coaches, 136

Lindsay, John V., 144–45, *148*, 150, 159, 160–61

Lindsay, Joseph, 149

"Little Wagner Act," 87

Long Island Rail Road: 1966 purchase by New York State, 160; 1966 transit strike and, 147; M series cars, 141; New York City's 1952 purchase of the Rockaway Beach Line, 109; takeover by the Metropolitan Transportation Authority, 161, 162; World's Fair service, 14, 137, *138*

Loos, Theodore, 84, 85, 86

Low-V subway car, *15*

M15 bus route, 57

M104 bus route, *55*

MABSTOA. See Manhattan and Bronx Surface Transit Operating Authority

MacDonald, John, 36, 37

Mack buses: "Bingham Macks," 58n6, 70–71; model C45, 38, *57*, *135*; model C50, *57*, 99; operated by East Side Omnibus, 32; purchased by Surface Transportation, *40*, *118*, *119*; purchased by the Board of Transportation in 1947–1949, 38, 50, *52*, 57–58, 68, *69*; purchased in New York's streetcar-to-bus conversion before World War II, 35, *40*

Maclean-Grove-Shephared Construction Company, 155–56

MacMahon, Douglas, 149

Manhattan: 1941 bus strike, 20–21; 1948 transit fare increase and, 63; bus operations (*see* Fifth Avenue Coach Company; Fifth Avenue Coach Lines; Fifth Avenue Coach/Surface Transit; New York City Omnibus Corporation); elevated lines, 4–5; elimination of the Third Avenue elevated, 111–16; express bus service to outlying boroughs, 161–62, *163*, 165; first subway in, 59–60; private to public bus transition in 1948, 56–58; streetcar operators, 16–17, 31–32

Manhattan and Bronx Surface Transit Operating Authority (MABSTOA), 133–35

Manhattan Bridge, 6, 152

Manhattan Bus Division, 56–58

Manhattan Railway Company, 111

Market Street Railway (San Francisco), 62

mass transit: LaGuardia's attitude toward, 1–2; overview of changes from 1940 to 1968, 162–66; trend of becoming public sector responsibilities, *12*, 13–14

McAneny, George, 60

McDonald Avenue Line, 71, 72–73

McDonald–Vanderbilt streetcar, *47*

McQuistion, Victor, 37, 38

Meissner, Edwin, *88*

Memorandum of Understanding, 83

Metro-North, 140, 141, 147, 161

Metropolitan Avenue Line, *13*

Metropolitan Commuter Transportation Authority (MCTA), 160, 162

Metropolitan Transit Authority (Boston), 62

Metropolitan Transportation Authority (MTA): creation of, 159–61, 162; elimination of the Myrtle elevated, 79; express bus service, 162; "Program for Action," 158; takeover of private bus operations in Bronx, Brooklyn, and Queens, 89

Metropolitan Transportation District, 160

Miss Subways, 93, *93*, *104*

Moran, Eugene, 81

Moreland, John, 129

Morris Avenue streetcar, 35

Moses, Robert, 29, 159

Mother Hale Depot, *24*

Motor Coach Employees Fraternity (Chicago), 20

Motormen's Benevolent Association (MBA), 84, 85, 86

M series commuter cars, 141

MTA. *See* Metropolitan Transportation Authority

M train, 5, 158

multiple unit door control (MUDC) elevated cars, 111

Municipal Railway (San Francisco), 62

Myrtle Avenue elevated, 6, *44, 45,* 46, 75, 78–79

Nassau Street subway, 152

National Labor Relations Act, 19

New England Thruway, 29

New Haven Railroad, 25–26

"New Look" GM buses, 73, *91,* 92. *See also* "Fish-bowl" buses

New Orleans, 94

New York, New Haven, and Hartford Railroad, 25–26

New York, Westchester, and Boston Railroad, 25–26

New York Central Railroad, 140, 146–47

New York City: 1962 seizure of Fifth Avenue Coach/Surface Transit's buses and garages, 132–33; impact of the 1966 transit strike, 146–48; overview of mass transit from 1940 to 1968, 162–66; shortfall in transit revenues between 1913 and 1931, 2

New York City Corporation Counsel, 156

New York City Omnibus Corporation (NYCO): 146th Street and Lenox Avenue depot, *24;* 1955 NYCTA plan for bus privatization and, 87; combined Fifth Avenue/NYCO operation, 8, 117 (*see also* Fifth Avenue Coach Company); elimination of the Third Avenue elevated and, 115; fare increases, 23; GMC buses, *118;* history of, 16, 17–18; labor relations, 18–24; Queens bus operations in 1947, 52; Yellow Coach buses, *18, 32, 118*

New York City Transit Authority (NYCTA): 1953 subway fare increase and introduction of tokens, 81–82; 1966 transit strike, 95, 145–50; background to the creation of, 80–81; B Division, 140, 165; bus improvements, *91,* 92–93; Chrystie Street Connection, 151–58; creation of, 1, 159; elimination of the Third Avenue elevated and, 113, 115; express bus service, 162, *163;* financial problems and the formation of the Metropolitan Transportation Authority, 159–61; five-person body, 81, 82; Great Northeast Blackout, 94–95; increased transit usage in the 1960s, 93; IND–BMT connections in the 1950s, 90–91, 100–110; labor relations, 82–87, 143–44, 161; MABSTOA and, 133–35; Miss Subways, 93, *93;* planned privatization of bus and trolley lines, 87, 89; replacement

of obsolete subway equipment, *88,* 89–90; responsibilities of, 81, 159; special trains to the Polo Grounds, 93–94; subway route expansions, 90–92; three-membered salaried panel, 87, 89; transit fares under, 94; West Side IRT Improvement Project, 122–28; World's Fair subway service, 137–38

New York City Transit System, 1

New York Mets, 138–39

New York Railways (NYR), 8, 16

New York State Public Authorities Law, 133, *134*

New York State Public Service Commission, 41, 49

New York Times: on the 1941 agreement for the employment of black transit workers, 22; on the 1941 bus strike, *20;* on the 1948 transit fare increase, *63, 64, 65;* on the 1957 wildcat subway motormen's strike, 84–85; on the 1962 transit strike, *131,* 132, *134;* on the 1968 transit contract, *161, 162;* on air-conditioned subway cars, 165; on the Chrystie Street Connection, *157;* on William Cimillo, *39,* 41; on the closing of Brooklyn's Lexington Avenue elevated, 77–78, *79;* on the Dyre Avenue subway extension, 26, *27;* on the end of elevated lines across the Brooklyn Bridge, *48;* on the end of the Broadway–Kingsbridge streetcar, 36; on R 32 subway cars, 139, *140;* Samuel Rosoff's obituary, 56n4; on subway unification, 2, 3; on the West Side IRT Improvement Project, 127, *128*

New York Times Magazine, 23, 39, 61

New York World's Fair (1939–1940), 14–15,

New York World's Fair (1964–65), 137–38, 142

nickel fare: 1948 fare increase, 62–66; Dual Contracts agreements and, 2n3, 59; duration of, 59; LaGuardia's support for, 1–2, 12, 61; as a political issue, 3, 60–61; revenue problems and, 60, 61–62; revenues during World War II, 12

Ninety-First Street Station, 122

Ninety-Sixth Street Station, 122, 123, 125–26, 128

Ninth Avenue elevated, *5,* 111

North Shore Bus Company, 51, *52,* 53–54

Norton, Henry K., 81

Nostrand Avenue Station (Lexington Avenue El), *76*

N train, 107

Number 1 Broadway Line, *88*

Number 1 train, *55,* 123, 127

Number 2 train, 30, 123, 127–28

Number 3 train, 123, 127–28

Number 5 train, 30

Number 7 train, 137, 139

Number 9 train, 123
Number 14 train, 156, 157
Number 15 Jackson Heights bus route, 98, 99
Number 15 train, 156
NX train, 156, 158
NYCO Division (New York City Omnibus), 117
NYCTA. *See* New York City Transit Authority

Ocean Avenue Line, *10*
O'Dwyer, William, 59, 62, 68, *69*, 83
O'Grady, Joseph, 89, 139
180th Street–Bronx Park Station, 122n1
149th Street–Third Avenue subway station, *116*
104th Street–Oxford Avenue Station, *108*
103rd Street Station, *126*

Palmer, Arthur, 159
Park Row Terminal, 42, *44, 45,* 46–47
PATH trains, 148
PATH tunnels, 155
Patterson, Charles, *88, 89,* 94, *104, 154*
PCC streetcars. *see* President's Conference Commit-
    tee streetcars
Pelham Parkway Station, *30*
Penn Central Railroad, 141
Penn Station, *146,* 147, 148
Peter Witt type streetcars, *10, 11, 73*
Philadelphia, 94
Philadelphia Transportation Company, 96, 99
plow pit, *32*
plows, 16n1, *32*
Port Authority Bus Terminal, 148
Port Authority of New York and New Jersey, 81
Port of New York Authority, 81
Powell, Adam Clayton, Jr., 22
President's Conference Committee (PCC) streetcars,
    7–8, *13,* 33n3, 47, *67,* 71, *72, 73*
Pressman, Gabe, *91*
Price, Robert, 149
"Program for Action" (MTA), 158
Prospect Park accident (1918), 3
Prospect Park and Coney Island Railroad, 43, 45
Prospect Park IND subway branch, 100
Pullman-Standard Company, 141

Q36 bus route, *53*
Q72 Junction Boulevard bus line, 89
QB train, 156
QJ train, 156, 157, 158

Q train, 158
Q type wooden elevated line cars, 79
Queen Mary double-deck buses, *17,* 96–98, 99
Queens, 1948 transit fare increase and, 63; 1966
    transit strike and, 145, 147; bus and trolley
    operations in 1947, 51; private to public bus
    transition, 52–55, 56; special trains to the Polo
    Grounds, 93–94
Queensboro Bridge, *4*
Queensboro Bridge shuttle, 74
Queens Boulevard bus, 147
Queens Boulevard subway, *93,* 103–4, *105,* 106–7, 109
Queens Bus Division, 54–55, 56, 83, 86
Queens-Nassau Transit, 52
Queens Surface Corporation, 52n, 74
Quill, Michael: 1962 strikes against Fifth Avenue
    Coach/Surface Transit and, *130,* 131, 132; 1965
    negotiations with John Lindsay, 144–45; 1966
    transit strike and, 145, 146, *148,* 149; death and
    funeral of, 149–50; heart attack, 146; negotia-
    tions with Robert Wagner, 19; negotiations with
    the NYCTA, 143; opposition to the elimination
    of the Third Avenue elevated, *114;* support for
    work rule efficiencies, 84–85; TWU's 1960 dispute
    with Fifth Avenue Coach Lines and, 120; wildcat
    strikes by subway motormen and, 84, 85–86

railroads: industrial union model and, 86–97; steam
    railroads in Brooklyn, 43, 45
Raskin, A. H., 85–86
Rauchwerger, Joseph, 53, 54
Reconstruction Finance Corporation, 8
"Redbird" subway cars, 139
retirement benefits, 161
Ritchie, John, 20
Riverdale Transit Company, 162
RJ train, 156, 157
Rockaway Beach Line, 109
Rockaway Park, 109
Rockaway Parkway Station, *91*
Rockaway subway line, 90–91
Rockefeller, Nelson, 133, 135, 159–61
Rogers, Hugo, 36
Rosoff, Samuel "Subway Sam," 56
RR train, 107, 156, 157
R series subway cars: operated by BMT, 90, 106, 107;
    operated by IND, *15,* 89–90, 106, 107, 158, 160;
    operated by IRT, *88, 89,* 90, *116,* 123; R1-9 cars, *15,*
    89, 90, 106, 107, 158; R11 cars, 90, 139; R12, R14,

R series: R15, and R16 cars, 90; R17 cars, 116; R22 cars, 123; R27-30 cars, *30, 88,* 90; R32 cars, 90, 139–42, *155*; R33–36 cars, 137–38, 139, *164*; R38 cars, 90; R40 cars, 90, 160, *163*; R42 cars, 90, *163*

R train, 107

San Francisco, 62, 94
Scannell, Daniel, *150*
Schenck Transportation Company, 54
Schumach, Murray, 61
Sea Beach Express, 106
Sea Beach Line, 107, 152, 153
Second and Third Avenue elevated, *5*
Second Avenue elevated, *4, 5,* 111
Second Avenue subway, 90, 91, 100, 101, 112, 116, 153, 165
Seventh Avenue Express subway, 30, 122
Seventh Avenue Local subway, 122–23
Seventh Avenue streetcar, *47*
Seventy-Second Street Station, 123, *124*
Shea Stadium, 138–39
Sixth Avenue: Chrystie Street Connection and, 154–55, 156
Sixth Avenue Concourse Line, 156
Sixth Avenue elevated, 111
Sixth Avenue subway, 151, 152
Sixth Avenue–Washington Heights Local subway, 156
Sixtieth Street Tunnel, *103, 104,* 105
Sixty-Third Street Tunnel, 158
Slater, Steven, 41
Smith Street–Coney Island Avenue streetcar, 7
snow plows, *18*
South Bay Corporation, 136
St. George Ferry Terminal, 49, 52
St. Johns Place trolley coach, *71, 73*
St. Louis Car Company, 68, *71, 88,* 137, 141
stainless steel subway cars, 137, 139–42
Standard subway cars, *14,* 105–6
Staten Island: 1948 transit fare increase and, 63; 1966 transit strike and, 147; private to public bus transition, 49–50, 52
Staten Island Bus Division, 50, 56, 83, 86
Staten Island Coach Company, 49
Staten Island Rapid Transit, 147
steam railroads: in Brooklyn, 43, 45
Steinway Omnibus, *52*
Steinway Transit Corporation, 74, 162
storage battery streetcars, 33

streetcars and trolleys: 1948 fare increase, 62–66; 1950 fare increase, 66; 1955 NYCTA plan for the privatization of, 87, 89; across the Brooklyn Bridge, 6, 42–48; in the Bronx, *40*; in Brooklyn, 7–8, 67; collection shoes, 16n1; double-ended, 35n5; Electric Railway President's Conference Committee, 7; LaGuardia's opposition to, 7, 8; in Manhattan, 16–17, 31–32; Peter Witt type cars, *10, 11, 73*; plows, 32; in Queens in 1947, *51*; storage battery cars, 33; Third Avenue Railway Company, 31–32. *See also* streetcar-to-bus conversion
streetcar-to-bus conversion: in Brooklyn, 6–10, 67–74; impact of World War II on, 35; LaGuardia and, 34–35; in other US cities, 67; Third Avenue Transit and, 31, 33, 34–37
strikes: 1941 strike against Fifth Avenue Coach-New York Omnibus, 20–21; 1946 strike against Isle Transportation, 50; 1962 strikes against Fifth Avenue Coach/Surface Transit, 129–30, 131–32, *133*; 1966 transit strike, 95, 145–50; wildcat strikes by subway motormen, 84–86
subway cars: air-conditioned, 90, 139, 140, 141, *163,* 165; "Brightliners," 141; dimensions, 151; IRT 1940 car fleet, *15*; Low-V unit, *15*; overview of purchases and changes from 1947 to 1968, 164, 165; "Redbirds," 139; R series (*see* R series subway cars); Standard cars, *14,* 105–6; Triplex unit, *14*
subway motormen: wildcat strikes, 84–86
subways: 1948 fare increase, 62–66; 1966 transit strike, 95; Chrystie Street Connection, 90, 91, 103, 151–58, 165; Dual Contracts agreements, 59; free transfers between a bus and subway, *91*; Great Northeast Blackout, 94–95; historical overview, 59–60; identification of trains and routes, 165; Miss Subways, 93, *93, 104*; nickel fare (*see* nickel fare); NYCTA route expansions, 90–92; NYCTA's replacement of obsolete equipment in the 1950s, *88,* 89–90; overview of changes from 1940 to 1968, 162–66; replacement of elevated lines in Manhattan and Brooklyn, 4–5; service to Shea Stadium, 138–39; special trains to the Polo Grounds, 93–94; West Side IRT Improvement Project, 122–28; World's Fair subway service, 14–15, 137–38. *See also* Brooklyn-Manhattan Transit Company; Independent Subway System; Interborough Rapid Transit Company
subway station platforms: extensions as a part of the West Side IRT Improvement Project, 122, 123–24, 127

Subway Sun, 95, 109, 126

subway-to-surface line transfers. *See* transfers

subway turnstiles, 81

subway unification: 1939–1940 World's Fair and, 14–15; Board of Transportation's purchase of the BMT and IRT in 1940, 1; elimination of Brooklyn elevated lines and, 46–47; elimination of the Third Avenue elevated and, 111; financial issues, 11–12; historical background, 3; labor relations issues, 10–11; LaGuardia and, 1–2; operating issues, 3–10; shortfall in fare revenues and, 2; trend of mass transit becoming public sector responsibilities and, *12, 13–14*

Surface Transit, Incorporated, 117–21. *See also* Fifth Avenue Coach/Surface Transit

Surface Transportation System: 1948 bankruptcy, 41; 1955 NYCTA plan for bus privatization and, 87; buses purchased by, *40, 41, 118, 119*; elimination of the Third Avenue elevated and, 115; financial problems, 37; founding of, 31, 33; purchased by Fifth Avenue Coach Lines, 41, 117; Third Avenue Railway and, 16–17

Taylor, George, 145

Teamsters Local 643, 150

Third Avenue Bridge, 35

Third Avenue elevated (Manhattan), 5, 111–16, *112*

Third Avenue Line elevated (Bronx), 4

Third Avenue Railway Company: history of, 31–32; labor relations, 33–34; streetcar-to-bus conversion, 31, 33, 34–37; TWU and, 19

Third Avenue Railway System, 16–17

Third Avenue streetcar (Brooklyn), *10, 11, 13, 55*

Third Avenue Transit System: 1949 bankruptcy action, 37–38; William Cimillo incident, 39, 41; labor relations, 38–39, 41; streetcar-to-bus conversion, 31, 36–40

Thirty-Fourth Street Station (Third Avenue Elevated), *113*

tokens, 81–82

Tompkins Avenue Station, *78*

transfers: 1948 transit fare increase and, 63, *64, 65–66*; from Brooklyn buses to IND subways, 48, 70; free transfers, *91*; intercompany, 4; interdivisional, 4; on MABSTOA routes, 136; troubles in 1962 with Fifth Avenue Coach/Surface Transit, 130, 134

Transit, 8, 109

transit fares: 1948 increase, 62–66; 1950 increase, 66; 1952 increase, 80; 1953 subway fare increase and

the introduction of tokens, 81–82; under the NYCTA, 94; in other US cities, 62, 80, 94; revenues during World War II, 12; shortfall in revenues between 1913 and 1931, 2; Third Avenue Transit's labor issues and, 38–39. *See also* bus fares; nickel fare

Transit Labor Board, 145

Transit Research Corporation (TRC), 7

transit workers: 1962 layoff by Fifth Avenue Coach/ Surface Transit, 130–31; 1962 strikes against Fifth Avenue Coach/Surface Transit, 129–30, 131–32, *133*; equal employment agreement for black transit workers, 22–24; retirement benefits, 161; TWU hegemony in the representation of, 83; Wagner Act and, 19. *See also* labor relations; strikes

Transportation Corporation of America, 130

Transport Workers Union (TWU): 1960 dispute with Fifth Avenue Coach Lines, 120–21; 1962 strikes against Fifth Avenue Coach/Surface Transit, 129–30, 131–32, *133*; 1966 transit strike, 145–46, *145–50, 147, 148–49*; dispute on the conversion of double-deck buses to one-man operation, 96–97; founding of, 19; hegemony in the representation of New York transit workers, 83; industrial union model and, 82–83, 86–87; Memorandum of Understanding with the Board of Transportation, 83; opposition to the elimination of the Third Avenue elevated, *114*, 115; Mike Quill's 1965 negotiations with John Lindsay, 144–45; relations with the NYCTA, 83, 143–44, 161; strikes and agreements with Fifth Avenue Coach-New York Omnibus companies, 19–24; subway unification and, 10, 11; Third Avenue Railway Company and, 34; Third Avenue Transit and, 39; United Motormen's Division, 86; Robert F. Wagner and, 87; wildcat strikes by subway motormen, 84–86

Tremont Avenue streetcar, *40*

Triboro Coach, *52*, 89

Triborough Bridge and Tunnel Authority (TBTA), 81, 159, 160, 161

Triplex subway car, *14*

trolley coaches, 67, 68, 73

trolleys. *See* streetcars and trolleys

Tunneling to the Future (Derrick), 60

Twin Coach Company buses, 8, 35, *40, 41, 53, 55*, 68, *69, 71*

240th Street Yard, *88*

TWU. *See* Transport Workers Union

United Motormen's Division, 86
United Negro Bus Strike Committee, 22–23

Vanderbilt, Amy, *91, 92*–93

wages: 1941 bus strike in Manhattan and, 21
Wagner, Robert F., *108*; 1957 wildcat strike by
    subway motormen and, 86; 1962 strikes against
    Fifth Avenue Coach/Surface Transit and, 129, 132;
    creation of MABSTOA and, 135; NYCTA's
    three-member salaried panel and, 89; Rockaway
    Line opening 1956, *108*; relationship with labor,
    87, 143; West Side IRT Improvement Project
    and, 127
Wagner Act, 19
War Production Board, 47
Weinberg, Harry, 129, 130–31, 132, 135, 136
Weissman, Lawrence, 136
West 5th Street Depot (Coney Island), *13*
Westchester County: Fifth Avenue Coach routes,
    135–36
Westchester Street Transportation Company, 135–36
West End subway, 152–53, 156
West Farms Square, *133*
West Side IRT Improvement Project, 122–28

White Motor Company, 50, *52,* 99
Wicks, Arthur H., 10
Wicks law, 11
wildcat strikes: by subway motormen, 84–86
Willets Point Station *138*
Williamsburg Bridge, 45, 79, 94–95, 153, 158
Willis Avenue–125th Street streetcar, 35
Willis Avenue Bridge, 35
Windels, Paul, 61, 81
wooden elevated line cars, 79
World's Fair (1939–1940), 14–15,
World's Fair (1964–65), 137–38, 142
World War II: impact on streetcar-to-bus conver-
    sion, 35; impact on transit system upgrading, 12;
    revenues from the nickel fare during, 12
WPA Guide to New York City, 3, 60

Yellow Coach buses: model 735 double-deck bus,
    97; model 5401, 98–99; purchased
    by New York City Omnibus, *18, 32, 118*;
    purchased for Third Avenue Railways prewar
    streetcar-to-bus conversion, 35, *41. See also*
    General Motors Corporation buses

Zelano, Frank, 86